Managing for Marketing Excellence

Ian Chaston
Principal Lecturer in Marketing
Polytechnic South West Business School

McGRAW-HILL BOOK COMPANY

London · New York · St Louis · San Francisco · Auckland
Bogotá · Caracas · Hamburg · Lisbon · Madrid · Mexico
Milan · Montreal · New Delhi · Panama · Paris · San Juan
São Paulo · Singapore · Sydney · Tokyo · Toronto

Published by
McGRAW-HILL Book Company (UK) Limited
Shoppenhangers Road, Maidenhead, Berkshire SL6 2QL, England
Telephone 0628 23432
Fax 0628 35895

British Library Cataloguing in Publication Data
Chaston, Ian
  Managing for marketing excellence.
  1. Marketing
  I. Title
  658.8

ISBN 0-07-707237-5

Library of Congress Cataloging-in-Publication Data
Chaston, Ian.
  Managing for marketing excellence/Ian Chaston.
    p. cm.
  ISBN 0–07–707237–5.
  1. Marketing – Management. I. Title.
HF5415.13.C512 1990
658.8–dc20

12345B 93210
Typeset by Computape (Pickering) Ltd, North Yorkshire.
Printed and bound in Great Britain by
Page Bros (Norwich) Ltd

In memory of my parents
Cecil and Joan Chaston

CONTENTS

Preface   **xi**

1   Managing the marketing process   **1**

The post-war corporate heroes   1
Adoption of the marketing-orientated philosophy   2
How others sometimes view the marketing operation   3
Humble Products Ltd   3
Defining the marketing task   6
Potential for conflict   8
References   11

2   The business environment — source of change and opportunity   **13**

Components of the business environment   13
The customer   14
The competition   17
Intermediaries   18
Suppliers   20
Environmental turbulence   21
Managing information   23
References   24

3   Internal capability and vulnerability   **25**

Functional interrelationships   25
Marketing capability   27
Product as a dominant factor   27
Price as a dominant factor   27

Promotion as a dominant factor 28
Place as a dominant factor 29
Financial capability 30
Manufacturing capability 33
Technological capability 34
Managerial capability 35
References 36

4 Selecting appropriate strategies 38

Market leadership 38
Segmentation strategies 41
Product portfolio strategies 42
Corporate capability strategies 46
An illustration of the directional strategy approach 50
References 52

5 Managing new products 53

What is a 'new' product? 53
A management model for new product development 53
Marketeers and innovation 55
Organizational barriers to innovation 56
Idea generation and organizational structure 57
Innovative problem-solving 60
Working in teams 62
New product success 63
References 63

6 Marketing tactics 65

The lesson of the First World War 65
Non-confrontational attack 67
Holding on to what you have 70
References 74

7 Pricing, promotion and distribution decisions 76

Marketing mix and corporate strategy 76
Pricing decisions 77
Monitoring the validity of the price decision 80
Sales promotion — a tactical pricing strategy 80
Promotion — process and planning 83
Selection of the promotional mix 85
Distribution decisions 86
Managing the distribution process 88

Marketing mix assessment 89
References 90

8 Forecasting and assessing performance **92**

Adequacy of analysis 92
Forecasting sales 93
New products 95
Managing the future 96
Enhanced accuracy 97
Marketing expenditure 97
Model building and the planning process 100
Balance sheet performance 102
References 105

9 Performance control **107**

From information to control 107
Limited control 108
Diagnostic control 109
Diagnostic financial variance control 111
Diagnostic managerial accounting control 111
Integrative control 116
Proactive control 117
References 119

10 Integrating the manufacturing and marketing operations **121**

The interrelationships between manufacturing and
    marketing 121
Cost of goods 123
Overhead absorption 124
Economic order quantity 126
Just in time 127
Total quality management 128
Product improvement programmes 129
Product development programmes 130
Capacity planning 133
References 137

11 The 'Ps' and 'Q' of service marketing **139**

Service Marketing 139
The contribution of marketeers to service industries —
    the new 'Ps' 141
Acceptance of marketeers in service organizations 142

The customer care concept for delivering quality in
    service markets   144
Marketeers and customer care   145
Remedying quality problems   147
Further development of the customer care system   148
References   149

12   Managing change   **151**

The need for change   151
Marine Circuits Ltd   151
Gaining acceptance for the need for change   153
Understanding the defenders   154
Gaining support for a proposal of change   155
Marine Circuits — strategic change   156
Resolving conflict   157
Marine Circuits — handling opposition   159
Implementing the change   160
The marketeer as a manager   160
The marketeer as an effective manager   161
Organizational culture   162
References   163

Glossary   **164**

Index   **170**

PREFACE

During the fifties and sixties, management theorists predicted that the marketing function would become a vital contributor in sustaining the success of both private and public sector organizations. Over the last few years, however, a number of academics have expressed concern that, even in the late eighties, the importance of marketing has still not been totally accepted.

Attempts to explain this situation have tended to focus upon the issue that senior managers do not appreciate the benefits of adopting a marketing-orientated approach across the entire organization. No doubt this perspective may be valid in some instances. Nevertheless, management theorists do seem to ignore an alternative scenario: namely, poorly managed marketing departments have contributed little to corporate performance and senior managers who experience this situation have concluded that 'less, not more, emphasis or resources for the marketing operation' is a safer operating philosophy.

As an academic who previously worked as a marketeer for a large US corporation, I am in the privileged position of having time to reflect on earlier managerial performance. In hindsight, it is apparent that some of my decisions showed an inadequate appreciation of the vital importance of integrating the marketing role with the activities of other departments within the organization. Furthermore, my contribution could have been enhanced if I had developed more fully my interpersonal skills. Subsequent contact with managers from other disciplines during consultancy, delivering management training and undertaking research, has caused me to realize that some marketeers exhibit similar weaknesses during their attempts to manage the marketing process effectively. It would seem, therefore, that there is a need for marketeers and managers from other disciplines to gain further understanding of:

- how marketing staff can enhance their contribution to overall corporate performance;
- the skills marketeers must acquire in order to achieve the required level of excellence in managing the marketing process.

The text examines quality of performance in relation to the issues of environmental analysis, capability assessment, strategic planning, optimizing the marketing mix, forecasting, control, interdepartmental integration and managing change. Concepts are presented by relating marketing theory to examples of both reasonable and dubious management practice.

The materials presented have been developed with the aim that the text will be of benefit to participants in undergraduate or postgraduate programmes for non-marketing specialists and to supplement the main text used in marketing management programmes. It is also hoped that the materials will be of assistance to managers from all disciplines seeking to gain further understanding of how the marketing process can be managed effectively.

Some academics and marketing managers may feel that at times the text deals rather harshly with current practices. It is perhaps worth pointing out to these readers that recent research by Lonsdale Research in conjunction with *Marketing Week* revealed that a large proportion of UK marketeers have doubts about the impact of their role on corporate performance ('When the research addicts surveyed their own intimate secrets', V. Matthews, *The Daily Telegraph*, 3 May 1989). For example, 67 per cent of respondents felt that their jobs contributed nothing or very little to society. To these readers I offer my apologies and would be pleased to receive materials that vitiate my criticisms of the managerial weaknesses of some marketeers.

On the other hand, managers from other functional disciplines may be aware of situations where marketeers have weakened the overall performance of the organization. Should they be willing to share such scenarios, I would be most grateful to receive more information as this will be of assistance in developing additional theories about the manner in which marketeers can be persuaded to fulfil their responsibility to achieve managerial excellence.

Ian Chaston

CHAPTER ONE

MANAGING THE MARKETING PROCESS

THE POST-WAR CORPORATE HEROES

As the industrial nations embarked on the rebuilding of their economies after the Second World War, management theorists began to focus on the question of how companies can continue to be successful. A widely promoted theory was that corporate performance could be improved by adopting a 'marketing-orientated' business philosophy. This approach was based on the assumption that companies could more readily achieve their financial goals by, firstly, determining the needs of their customers and then satisfying these through providing appropriate products or services. The marketing-orientated philosophy was presented as superior to the more traditional concept of creating a product and then seeking out sufficient customers.[1]

As the consumers in the western world began to enjoy real gains in income during the fifties and sixties, marketing-orientated companies effectively exploited the growing demand for products such as cars, television sets, frozen food and foreign travel. Initially most companies established marketing as a functional department having authority equal to that of other groups such as production or finance. However, as evidence was accumulated on the important contribution marketing could make to corporate performance, some marketeers began to propose that their role should be recognized as being the most important within the organization. In support of their proposal they pointed out that satisfying customer needs was paramount, for without customers there could be no company. The more ardent disciples of the new 'religion' went as far as to suggest that marketing was really the centre of the corporate universe around which the less vital satellite roles of production, finance, administration and personnel should all revolve.

By the seventies some observers began to question whether, in a world of declining resources, population growth and inflation, this new marketing management approach was irresponsible, given its excessive emphasis on uncontrolled consumption.[2] As eloquent and persuasive advocates of their own cause, the reaction of marketeers was predictable. If conservation was a developing market need, then the marketeers would be quite willing to respond to this new trend by expanding their responsibilities to encompass the future well-being of society in general. This broader approach was packaged under the phrase of adopting a 'societal marketing' philosophy.[3]

ADOPTION OF THE MARKETING-ORIENTATED PHILOSOPHY

Despite the intuitive appeal of the marketing concept, there is evidence that many organizations have yet, fully, to implement the philosophy.[4] One possible reason is that the corporate culture established by senior management places emphasis on short-term performance objectives such as high profitability or return on investment (ROI). These goals are unlikely to be met if plans have to be drastically revised in response to changing market needs.

Strong support for this explanation has been provided by the Peters and Waterman[5] research on the common characteristics of America's 'excellent companies'. This study demonstrated that successful companies were apparently those in which the management culture focuses upon highly flexible decision-making systems and the importance of the market place in determining future corporate plans.

Another possible reason why some companies have failed to adopt a marketing-orientated approach is that marketeers have in the past placed too great an emphasis on the importance of their role. This may cause a reduction of the resources available to other functional groups within the organization, who are then unable to undertake effectively the tasks for which they are responsible (e.g., if funds are allocated to a major advertising campaign, the manufacturing group may not gain approval to invest in the new machinery required to sustain processing operation productivity).[6]

Dominance of corporate activity is not unique to marketeers, but nevertheless this type of behaviour by one functional group is usually to the detriment of the organization's long-term performance.[7] Once it has occurred and the company has encountered major problems, senior management and staff from other departments become extremely resistant to any proposal from a marketeer. A recent example of this type of situation is provided by Shapiro[8] in a case study of the Wolverine Corporation, a manufacturer of flow controllers. To illustrate the anti-marketing attitude that can develop, the article quotes the Chief Executive Officer during a discussion on ways to improve corporate performance, as follows: 'I said market orientated, not marketing-orientated. It's unclear to me what we get from all the overheads we have in marketing ... Let's drive people to think about customers and the corporation as a whole, not just what's good for their own departments.'

HOW OTHERS SOMETIMES VIEW THE MARKETING OPERATION

As an individual involved in delivering post-experience courses, consultancy and management training programmes, the author has had numerous opportunities with line managers from other functional disciplines to raise the question of 'What are your views and experience of the capabilities of marketeers with whom you have worked?' In my own experience, which is shared by colleagues and associates in both North America and the UK, it is perceived by others that marketing personnel:

- are not held accountable for their actions;
- resist any attempts to place controls over their performance;
- are committed to actions which are of benefit to themselves, not the company;
- have insufficient understanding of business;
- lack financial management skills;
- rely on creativity without any analysis or diagnosis of available information when placed in a problem/solution situation;
- use market research to justify preconceptions;
- are out of touch with the industry of which the company is a part;
- often design plans to meet long-term objectives, whereas their actions usually only influence events over the short term;
- rarely seem to learn from their mistakes;
- leave other departments with insufficient financial resources due to the funding of their plans and staff budgets;
- in working with other departments, appear conceited, deaf to alternative proposals, uninformed, inexperienced and inflexible.

These attitudes have usually been formed by those who have worked in an organization that encountered problems in executing the marketing-orientated approach to business management. To illustrate how such adverse opinions are formed, therefore, it is worth examining the disguised case of Humble Products Ltd.

HUMBLE PRODUCTS LTD

The company was created by John Humble who felt there was a business opportunity in producing high-quality pickled vegetables such as onions,

Table 1.1 Promotional programme (£'000)

	Current performance	Budgeted future performance		
		Year 1	Year 2	Year 3
Sales	3000	3600	4200	5000
Cost of goods	1800	2160	2520	3000
Gross profit	1200	1440	1680	2000
(% Gross margin)	(40.0)	(40.0)	(40.0)	(40.0)
Marketing expense	60	300	300	300
Operating expense	740	810	870	950
Total expense	800	1110	1170	1250
Net profit	400	330	510	750
(% Net margin)	(13.3)	(9.2)	(12.1)	(15.0)

cabbage, beetroot and cauliflower. Within ten years of the business start-up, annual sales had reached £3m, with 40 per cent of sales under the Humble brand name to small retail outlets, 30 per cent to catering establishments and the balance of sales as own-label product to national supermarket chains.

Humble Products was acquired by a large, multinational conglomerate who wished to expand their involvement in the UK food industry. The new owners felt that the Humble management team placed too great an emphasis on production and were relatively weak in their approach to marketing. Hence, a new marketing director was brought in from the corporate planning department of the parent company. He commissioned a market research study which showed that in blind-taste tests, Humble products were rated by consumers to be of a higher quality than better known national brands. The marketing director concluded that this was sufficient evidence to support a strategy that focused on expanding the sale of the Humble brand in the UK retail sector. This strategy would be achieved by using increased promotional spending to heighten consumer awareness for the brand, while at the same time expanding the level of distribution, especially in the larger supermarket chains where the brand had only limited availability. To achieve the proposed expansion of the brand, the promotional budget was increased from £60 000 to £300 000 a year. The forecasted impact of the new spending level was as shown in Table 1.1.

In Year 1 of the new programme, sales did increase by 20 per cent as forecasted and the net profit target of £330m was achieved. The only variation from plan was that instead of the projected expenditure of £50 000 on sales promotion to provide temporary customer incentives (e.g., price pack, short-term price discounts and consumer coupons), it was found necessary to fund £120 000 of these programmes. The majority of this increase in sales promotion activity occurred during the last six months of the

Table 1.2 Budget vs actual performance

	Year 2 budget (£'000)	Year 2 actual (£'000)	% Variance (%)
Sales	4200	4100	−2.4
Cost of goods	2520	2580	+2.4
Gross profit	1680	1520	−9.5
(% Gross margin)	(40.0)	(37.0)	N/A
Total expense	1170	1170	0.0
Net profit	510	350	−31.3
(% Net margin	(9.2)	(8.5)	N/A

financial year when the marketing director decided there was a need for a 'short-term acceleration in sales velocity'. To fund these activities, without increasing total promotional spending, the marketing director cancelled the advertising campaign scheduled for the third and fourth quarters.

Sales in the early weeks of Year 2 were approximately 20 per cent lower than for the same period in the previous year, but later improved following the launch of new, larger pack sizes of the more popular vegetables. Nevertheless, to sustain an acceptable level of sales in the last six months of the year, it was again found necessary to switch funds from advertising to sales promotion. Efforts to expand distribution in the retail sector were frustrated because many of the national supermarket chains could not see the benefits of stocking Humble brand products. Retailers argued that this would only reduce sales of their own-label pickles which, in many cases, they were already buying from Humble.

Some of the major supermarket chains were also strongly critical of the heavy promotional discounts of 10–20 per cent on Humble brand products in the second half of Year 2. They felt that this type of programme was going too far in narrowing the price differential between their own-label products and the Humble brand. In the face of threats to cancel orders, the marketing director authorized a temporary price reduction on own-label products. The effect of this discount, coupled with the higher production costs of producing the larger pack sizes, was as shown in Table 1.2.

For some months the marketing director had been proposing that an even higher level of promotional spending was required if the company was to strengthen its market position. He suggested that to implement his programme without reducing profitability, Humble Products should introduce new product formulations that could significantly reduce the cost of goods and have little perceivable effect on product quality. This recommendation had been resisted by the other senior managers at Humble, but in the face of the Year 2 results and pressure from the parent company (caused in part by 'lobbying' of the parent company Board by the marketing director), the new formulations were introduced at the beginning of Year 3.

Table 1.3 Result of promotional programme

	Year 3 budget (£'000)	Year 3 actual (£'000)	% Variance (%)
Sales	5000	4300	− 14.0
Cost of goods	3000	2490	− 17.0
Gross profit	2000	1810	− 9.5
(% Gross margin)	(40.0)	(42.1)	N/A
Total expense	1250	1300	+ 4.0
Net profit	750	510	− 32.0
(% Net margin)	(15.0)	(11.9)	N/A

Both retail and catering wholesalers had placed larger than usual orders at the end of Year 2 to take advantage of the generous promotional discounts then available from Humble. A return to normal prices, combined with the higher than usual inventories now held by the wholesalers, caused sales in the first two months of Year 3 to slump. Faced with this situation, the marketing director decided to switch virtually the entire promotional budget out of advertising and into supporting sales promotion offers for the balance of the year.

Announcement of the promotional programme for the second quarter created further adverse response from own-label customers who could see the price differential between their goods and Humble brand virtually disappearing. The product reformulation had the potential to improve gross margin by 8 per cent. However, to dampen dissent among own-label customers, special discounts were made available and this action eroded a major proportion of the gross profit improvement generated by the reformulation.

Nine months into Year 3, the marketing director announced he was leaving to accept a position with a larger company in the food industry. He was therefore gone before the results of his activities were reflected by the results for the year (Table 1.3). In addition to the poor results, management at Humble were concerned by a small, but significant, level of complaints about a decline in the quality of Humble products, especially among their catering customers.

Over the next two years, despite changes of management invoked by the parent company, the situation at Humble showed little sign of improvement. Sales remained at the £4m level and net profitability at 11–12 per cent of sales. Then, during a period of 'strategic rationalization' by the parent group, John Humble was given the opportunity to buy back his company at a price that he could not refuse.

DEFINING THE MARKETING TASK

The Humble case is an illustration of how marketeers can act out their 'centre of the universe' role. The risk of this behaviour is that corporate performance

Figure 1.1 The marketing role.

is impaired because the marketeer favours a strategy based on growth through heavier promotional spending. This simplistic approach ignores the fact that the broader roles of marketing should be (*a*) to understand the needs and competitive conditions within the market and (*b*) to exploit those opportunities that are compatible with the internal capabilities of the organization.

Matching need to capability is a role which places marketing at the interface between the corporate and business environments. It is interesting to note that the model presented in Fig. 1.1 is the same as that proposed for marketing in management texts of the fifties and sixties. Later 'improvement' in the model by some academics and management consultants, which moved the marketing role to the centre of the organization, may have contributed to the acceptance of a flawed philosophy of allowing marketeers dominance over other departments.

Fulfilment of the marketing role involves the tasks described in Fig. 1.2. The goals associated with the marketing tasks are:

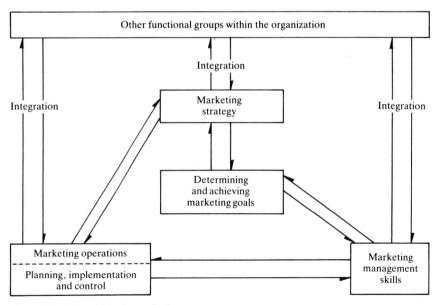

Figure 1.2 Tasks within the marketing process.

1. The 'strategic analysis' goal of identifying opportunities and threats in the business environment, then relating these to the capabilities within the organization.
2. The 'marketing planning' goal of employing the conclusions reached during the strategic analysis, in the preparation, implementation and control of appropriate marketing plans.
3. The 'corporate integration' goal of applying the managerial skills of communication, delegation, allocation of resources and staff development to establish an effective working relationship with other departments. This process helps to ensure that managers in all departments cooperate and thereby deliver the defined objectives of the entire organization.

A failure by marketeers in meeting any of the three goals of the marketing task can weaken corporate performance significantly. If all three goals remain unfulfilled, then the marketeer runs the risk of destroying the organization. In the Humble Products example, the marketing director's analysis of the market caused him to decide that the superior quality of the product could provide the basis of moving Humble from a specialist, up-market producer to a mass market operation. This conclusion ignored the strength of market acceptance established by existing national brands, their financial resources and the limited managerial capabilities of the Humble company. His incorrect strategic analysis provided the basis of an inappropriate marketing plan based on a simplistic assumption that heavier promotion and broader distribution could virtually double sales. Unfortunately, as evidence began to accumulate about the fundamental error of this plan, his reaction was to use short-term promotional activity to sustain forecasted sales. All this actually achieved was to mortgage future sales, as demonstrated by the poor performance upon a return to normal prices at the beginning of both Year 2 and Year 3. Managers in other departments recognized the long-term risk of sustaining profits through reducing the quality of the product, but the marketing director made no attempt to integrate his programmes with the rest of the management team at Humble. Instead he used the crisis of poor performance of Year 2 and pressure (instigated by him) from the parent company to force acceptance of the lower quality formulation to gain a transitory improvement in profitability. In these circumstances, where the marketing director has undermined the original cornerstone upon which the company was established, it comes as no surprise that Humble then entered a period of severe financial difficulty.

POTENTIAL FOR CONFLICT

In an increasingly volatile business environment one can anticipate differences of opinion between managers on how best to react to threats or opportunities presented to the organization. If participants approach such issues with the objective of seeking consensus on an optimal solution, progress will be achieved. However, where strongly differing opinions exist, coalitions will be formed and conflict may ensue.[9]

Marketeers may fail to recognize how feelings of insecurity caused by change within an organization may result in dissent between departments. For example, a move from a traditional production-orientated approach to that of a marketing-orientated company will be disturbing for individuals who perceive that this will change their role and responsibilities. As the agent of such a change, the marketeer should try to act as the catalyst for an integrated, cohesive response across the entire organization. However, in order to gain acceptance for the new philosophy, marketeers sometimes tend to be coercive to the point at which other departments join forces to defeat any change seen to originate from the marketing group.

In order to avoid conflict with other departments, the marketing group must ensure that their activities are seen to be effectively executed. One measurement of effectiveness is to see how many of the typical 'positive indicators' associated with an adequate managerial performance are to be found within an organization's marketing operation. Some examples of positive indicators are provided in Table 1.4.

Any marketing department which exhibits the range of positive indicators described in Table 1.1 is likely to discharge effectively its responsibilities to the organization of which it is a part. Furthermore, the overt willingness to actively cooperate with staff of other departments will ensure that marketing objectives are fully integrated with all other aspects of the corporate operations.

Where marketeers identify a lack of one or more key indicators it is their responsibility to remedy such weaknesses in order not to damage corporate performance. The complex nature of modern organizational structures, with heavy interdependence between operating groups, means that managers have an obligation to continuously assess their own group's effectiveness and to act before any problem has an impact on other areas of the organization. Current management theory emphasizes the importance of a team-based approach to the execution of tasks. No team can be effective, however, unless all members are willing to ensure that their performance is adequate.

The objectives of the balance of this text are, therefore, to examine various aspects of the marketing process so that marketeers and other management specialists can understand how to sustain corporate performance through managing for marketing excellence. As in the world of medicine, it is more effective to understand what constitutes a company's good health and to know how to prevent an adverse condition developing in the first place. For once a company is diagnosed as 'sick' due to poor marketing practice, a lengthy—and expensive—period of treatment may be needed before the 'patient' can be returned to good health.

Table 1.4 Positive indicators that are associated with adequate managerial performance within the marketing operation

Strategic role

1   Strategy based on carefully researched evidence of market conditions and not merely upon marketing staff's personal judgement.
2   Strategy only adopted following extensive discussion and review with other departments.
3   Strategy takes into consideration the weaknesses and strengths of competition.
4   Any significant shift in future strategy is based upon detailed analysis of why current corporate direction will become inappropriate.
5   If the new strategy places the company in a higher risk position, the degree of risk is clearly defined and a 'fall back' strategy is available if the new strategy proves not to be feasible.
6   Strategy is directly related to the internal capabilities of both the marketing group and/or other departments within the organization. Where any 'capability gap' is identified, there is proof that this can be remedied within the foreseeable future.

Marketing planning

1   Plan is based on realistic sales forecasts, with careful justification of all objectives.
2   Plan is based on clear relationships with prior year performance.
3   Annual plan is clearly compatible with the longer term overall corporate plan.
4   There are clear relationships with corporate sales objectives and overall market trends.
5   Sales objectives are based upon a careful assessment of the impact of competitive activity on corporate performance.
6   New product plans emphasize the development of fundamental changes in products capable of keeping the company ahead of competition and/or enter new market sectors.
7   Promotional programmes are based upon carefully researched objectives and include control systems to assess effectiveness when implemented.
8   Promotional and pricing policies reflect a full understanding of how intermediaries in the market system can influence corporate performance.
9   Pricing policies reflect carefully considered actions that are compatible with corporate profitability and ROI objectives.
10 The product line is continually being reviewed to ensure de-emphasis or timely discontinuation of slow-moving or loss-making items.

Implementation and control

1   Significant attention is given to analysing actual sales versus budget on a frequent basis throughout the financial year.
2   Any indication of poor actual sales performance immediately sets in motion remedial planning actions within the marketing group.
3   Promotional funds are not switched from other areas into short-term sales promotion activity unless it can be proved that this will not damage longer term performance or customer loyalty.
4   Competitive activity is carefully monitored and appropriate reaction implemented, especially in the case of newly emerging competitive threats.
5   There is a willingness to meet requests for information on market demand or internal costs which indicate a need to reconsider pricing decisions.
6   Any revisions in sales forecasts are based upon a careful analysis of market conditions and are accompanied by a detailed assessment of the implications of a revised forecast's impact on production schedules or finished goods inventories.
7   Granting of special prices to favoured customers is not permitted.

8   Discontinuation of slow-moving/loss-making products is completed within the time frame specified in the annual plan.
9   Distribution levels across all intermediaries are carefully monitored and there is an immediate response if the company is delisted by any major distributor.

Managing interdepartmental conflict
1   Other departments are kept updated on a regular basis.
2   When another department's error is discovered by the marketing department, this intelligence should be communicated in a diplomatic and constructive fashion.
3   Every possible effort is made to optimize finished goods stocks and avoid excess or out-of-stock situations.
4   Good cooperation is maintained with the credit control department over the management of accounts receivables and the avoiding of bad debt situations.
5   Careful attention is given to establishing realistic time-scales on projects involving input from other departments.
6   Where there is a difference of opinion with staff from other departments, the individuals concerned endeavour to settle the matter amicably and without involving senior staff except as a last resort.
7   It is assumed that any decline in gross profits is more likely to be caused by inadequate pricing than by rising production costs due to problems within the manufacturing operation.
8   Although willing to accept that a customer has grounds for making a product complaint, the marketing group's initial inclination is that of confidence in the company, and only accepting that the cause of the problem occurred prior to shipment after careful investigation of the facts.
9   It is accepted that the most likely cause of an incorrect or late shipment is that the marketing/sales group made an error when placing the order.
10 There is an immediate response to any reasonable requests for financial information by the accounting department.
11 Willing acceptance that any adverse variance in performance is a reality and not a reflection of incorrect accounting procedures.
12 It is understood that their requests for assistance from other departments will be given equal, not higher, priority by such departments relative to other demands also placed upon them.
13 Criticism of the marketing operation by other departments is accepted as probably valid, and constructive suggestions on ways to improve performance by sources outside the marketing operation are encouraged.

REFERENCES

1. P. Kotler, *Marketing Management—Analysis, Planning and Control*, 6th edn, Prentice-Hall, 1988.
2. M. L. Bell and C. W. Emery, 'The faltering marketing concept', *Journal of Marketing*, pp. 37–42, October 1971.
3. P. Kotler and G. Zaltmann, 'The growing responsibility of marketing', *Journal of Marketing*, vol. 34, p. 27, 1970.
4. P. Kotler, 'From sales obsession to marketing effectiveness', *Harvard Business Review*, pp. 67–75, November 1977.
5. T. J. Peters and R. J. Waterman, *In Search of Excellence*, Harper & Row, 1982.
6. R. C. Bennet and R. G. Cooper, 'Beyond the marketing concept', *Business Horizons*, pp. 76–83, June 1979.

7. A. C. Finlay and R. J. House, *Management Processes and Organisational Behaviour*, Scott Foresman, 1969.
8. B. L. Shapiro, 'What the hell is marketing orientated?', *Harvard Business Review*, vol. 88, pp. 119–125, 1988.
9. T. V. Bonoma, *The Marketing Edge*, Free Press, 1985.

CHAPTER TWO

THE BUSINESS ENVIRONMENT—SOURCE OF CHANGE AND OPPORTUNITY

COMPONENTS OF THE BUSINESS ENVIRONMENT

A visual representation (Fig. 2.1) of a typical market system shows the 'core' surrounded by the macroenvironment. Contained within the core are suppliers, producer companies, intermediaries and customers. Some producer companies may elect to deal directly with their customers (e.g., a boat builder constructing in-shore patrol craft for a government department) or use the services of an intermediary to provide customers with access to the product (e.g., the same boat builder who markets leisure craft to the general public through marine-based distributors in various parts of the country).

The macroenvironment contains variables such as technology or culture which may influence one or more elements within the core system (e.g., advances in carbon fibre technology which permit the boat builder to produce lighter, stronger hulls; a cultural shift in awareness about pollution which causes more customers in the leisure craft sector to favour yachts over power boats).

For a company to establish and sustain an effective marketing strategy, the marketing department must have a very detailed understanding of all the relationships that exist within the core and macroenvironment. This understanding will provide the basis for identifying opportunities that can be exploited, and threats that may have to be overcome. Without this knowledge companies may risk poor financial performance because they failed to identify a new threat within the business system, or they may find themselves unable to react to changes which ultimately lead to the company's failure.[1] Examples are the UK motorcycle industry in the 1960s when confronted with

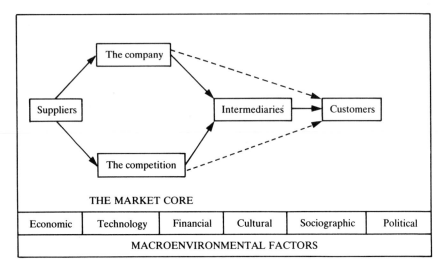

Figure 2.1 An example of a market system.

the competitive threat posed by Japanese products; and some UK stockbrokers following the restructuring of the City of London financial community in the aftermath of the 'Big Bang' in 1985 and 'Black October' in 1987.

THE CUSTOMER

Marketing departments will usually have acquired information on the current size of the market, the number of potential customers, customer per capita expenditure and the company's share of business within the market. Over the last 20 years, companies marketing consumer goods have recognized that many markets contain subgroups of customers (or 'segments') who have specific needs.[2] This situation will demand further data collection to provide a better understanding of their customer subgroups. A common form of analysis of these segments is to examine buyer behaviour in relation to customer profiles based on sociodemographic variables such as age, sex, marital status, income, education and occupation. More sophisticated approaches may involve the psychographic analysis of lifestyle or the use of computer-based multidimensional scaling to produce space maps (e.g., the selection of the 18- to 25-year-old male B, C1 and C2 sociodemographic group by the UK brewers launching new lager brands and the presentation of such products in the context of lifestyle situations with which this segment can identify).

Faced with this apparent wealth of information, it is not unreasonable for companies to assume that the marketing group has a very complete

Table 2.1 Forecast of the age profile in the UK as a percentage of total population

Age group	1980	2000	2025
>65	14.8	15.3	20.8
15–64	64.0	65.3	62.9
0–14	5.6	6.7	7.8

Source: Henley Forecasting Centre (1987)

understanding of how to exploit customer purchase patterns. In some cases, however, this research effort is directed towards measuring the current situation, and too little effort is made towards predicting potential change over the medium to long term.[3] One example is the impact of medical technology on the age profile of society in many countries. As shown by the forecast for the UK (Table 2.1), the over-65 age group will represent an increasingly large proportion of the population. Some companies have already responded to the implications of this situation (e.g., construction companies who have reduced their activities in the 'starter home' sector and expanded their involvement in building warden-controlled, apartment communities for retired couples). Nevertheless, many national brand consumer goods companies still direct virtually all their marketing resources towards the market sector containing housewives aged 18–45 with children.

Demographic trends are relatively easy to measure and thereby provide the basis for altering product development plans. Other potential changes in consumer behaviour may be more difficult to evaluate. Few companies, for example, appear to invest significant resources in research to understand cultural shifts in the marketplace. They only realize the error of their ways when sales have been lost to a competitor. The impact of the subsequent business problem is illustrated by the move to healthier eating which began in the mid-seventies. Some of the large, multinational corporations discounted this trend as a passing phase influencing the minority of consumers. These companies were then vulnerable to smaller, often regional, food processors who willingly moved to satisfy demand for 'natural' products. When these multinationals finally awoke to this new threat, they were forced to invest major sums in 'crash' programmes to develop and launch new natural foods to recapture the sales lost to the smaller organizations who had used entrepreneurial flair to exploit a change in customer behaviour.

It is only in the last two decades that companies in the industrial goods sector have begun to embrace a more marketing-orientated approach.[4] But here again there is a tendency to concentrate marketing resources on managing current market opportunities, on the assumption that today's important customers will continue to be the main source of sales in the

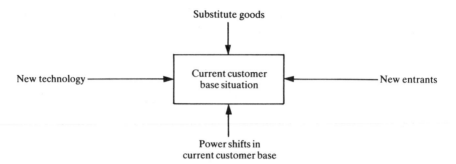

Figure 2.2 Forces of change in the customer base situation.

future. As Fig. 2.2 shows, however, there are a number of forces that could act to change the customer base within only a few years.

One way of demonstrating how the relative importance of customer groups can undergo dramatic change is to compare the entries in a trade directory with those published only five years earlier. Some companies will have disappeared and others who seemed very insignificant only a short time ago are now a major force in the market. It is therefore important for the marketeer to make a careful study of potential forces that can influence the future changes in the customer base. Consider, for example, British companies after the Second World War who continued to focus their efforts on supplying components to the European aircraft industry, ignoring the potential of US manufacturers such as Boeing to dominate world markets very rapidly.

Even if a component supplier is successful in predicting near-future changes in the importance of certain customers (such as the shift in market share dominance in the aircraft industry towards US corporations), it is also vital that the marketing department continues to monitor the environment to identify new entrants who could be the major customers of tomorrow. Many organizations failed to predict the arrival of the Japanese car manufacturers in world markets and, hence, were too late to become suppliers of components or services. Sustaining the aircraft example, will European or American component manufacturers be perceptive enough to gain sales from new entrants in the aerospace industry who are likely to emerge from within the Pacific Basin over the next few years.

On the issue of technology, one finds that marketeers are usually aware of the potential impact of this source of change on company products. They often quote the example of how the Swiss watch industry ignored the potential of the microchip to replace mechanical movements and thereby lost control of world markets to the more perceptive Japanese. Even seemingly very aware marketeers sometimes fail to extend their analyses to include forecasts of how technology may alter the future needs of their customers.

Especially in industrial markets, such weakness may affect a company because it is completely unprepared to meet a sudden shift in product demand.[5] As a recent example we can consider those companies who supplied traditional cables and wiring harnesses to the telecommunications industry, but did not recognize that their customers would begin to seek new components capable of exploiting the data transmission benefits of satellites and fibre optics.

An even more dramatic change can occur when the customer base decides to adopt substitute goods. Consider those consulting engineers and construction companies who had specialized in the building of nuclear power stations, only to find that, after disasters such as Three Mile Island and Chernobyl, some utility companies favoured a swift return to the more traditional forms of power generation. Suppliers who could contribute to the building of non-nuclear systems were able to cope with this reversal, but those organizations who had concentrated solely on involvement in the construction of nuclear power systems found that they were much less able to respond rapidly to this change in customer need.

THE COMPETITION

In his text on competitive strategy techniques, M. E. Porter[6] highlighted the dangers of allowing marketeers to be so preoccupied with end-user market trends that they ignore the potential threat posed by strategic change among their competitors.

As in the case of understanding customers, marketing departments often appear to be well informed about competition. Planning documents will contain detailed information on recent changes in brand share and results of usage and attitude studies showing weaknesses in other companies' products. Both these types of analysis are a description of the current situation and, in some cases, only apply to what was happening yesterday. Unless marketeers are prepared to make a much broader assessment of the competitive situation they are likely to ignore some of the major sources of future threat. These include new entrants (e.g., the success of the Japanese in entering the photocopier industry which many believed would always be dominated by the Xerox Corporation), suppliers to the industry who decide to acquire some of their customers' market (e.g., the Kuwait oil industry's entry into UK petrol retailing under the Q8 brand name), and customers who want to own their suppliers (e.g., supermarket chains who have taken over food processing companies).

Even in their analysis of existing competition, some marketeers make insufficient use of information sources outside of standard market research studies. Marketeers could learn a valuable lesson from the financial community on the benefits of studying annual accounts and shareholder reports as the basis for appraising the capability of companies. Financial analysts also exploit other sources of information to gain a more complete picture of the future prospects for a company. These include the perspectives of suppliers/intermediaries, publicity releases, announcement of capital investment programmes and recruitment advertising programmes. Given such a range of information it should be a danger signal to management if the marketing department only presents conclusions based on market share and customer surveys. For in today's highly competitive markets, this type of information is unlikely to provide the depth of knowledge that a company should hold on its competitors, if the marketing department is to be in a position to accurately predict new threats that may develop in the future.

INTERMEDIARIES

A not uncommon complaint from a salesforce is that their marketing department does not pay sufficient attention in their marketing plans to possible trends and changes among intermediaries. Some marketeers would argue that this type of activity is the responsibility of the salesforce. This is rather a naive perspective, however, for if the company is ineffectual in managing distribution channels, the customer will ultimately be unable to find a location at which to purchase the product.

A characteristic of many consumer goods markets is the increasing domination of distribution channels by a small number of multiple chainstore operations. The huge purchasing power of these retail groups means that they are able to demand special prices and promotional concessions in return for carrying the company's goods. Over the last ten years this situation has forced marketeers to work more closely with their national account group sales staff, and they have thereby begun to appreciate the importance of incorporating programmes on intermediary management into the marketing plan. Nevertheless, marketeers (as in the earlier discussion of response to competition) may not make sufficient effort to understand the potential impact on corporate performance of changes in channel structure of the type illustrated in Fig. 2.3. One possible situation is a change in attitude by intermediaries. This might be ignored by the marketing group until it is too late, and sales lost to a more perceptive competitor. The factor of concern here is that a buying behaviour shift by intermediaries usually occurs because they have noticed an attitude change at the end-user level before this has been identified by the supplier's own market research programmes. A recent example of this situation was the shift towards fresh fish and seafoods by consumers in the US and the UK. This trend was apparently ignored by most food manufacturers who continued to emphasize the marketing of frozen, processed products. As the national brand food companies were unable to meet this new need, retailers and caterers seeking fresh items were forced to find alternative suppliers.

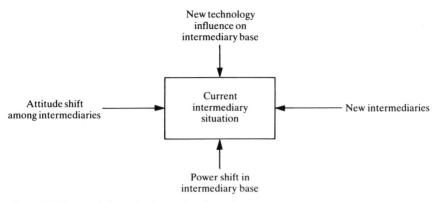

Figure 2.3 Forces of change in the market channel.

In developing marketing plans that encompass the future needs of intermediaries, marketeers must also be aware of power shifts in the distribution channels. A number of companies in Canada, for example, worked hard on developing their relationship with the dominant retailer Dominion Stores and virtually ignored the requirements of the much smaller, US-owned A&P group. When A&P subsequently acquired Dominion Stores, some companies found their services as suppliers were no longer required by the new owners and their products discontinued in the Dominion outlets.

A similar risk arises where companies ignore new entrants in distribution channels who at first seem small and therefore unimportant. The UK manufacturers of electrical appliances were slow to respond in the sixties to requests for support from the first retail discount operations. They felt that the new outlets could not provide the level of in-store sales service that manufacturers considered was necessary to merchandise their goods effectively. Some discount operations turned to overseas suppliers, such as the Italians, who were eager to gain a foothold in the UK market. In fact, one of the underlying reasons for the weakened position of UK white goods manufacturers in their home market over the last two decades was their original failure to recognize the potential power of discount operations.

A more recent example of the impact of new entrants is the increasing importance of mail order catalogue selling in the UK consumer market. Again some companies were slow to respond to this new factor and lost the opportunity to gain access to a new group of customers. The 1992 Single European Market is likely to be accompanied by the arrival from elsewhere in Europe of new retail groups in the UK. Observations suggest that some suppliers will not respond quickly enough and, as before, will fail to gain access to another group of new 'players' in the retail sector.

New technology also directly influences the operation of intermediaries.

At one time many retail groups were unwilling to permit manufacturers' representatives into their stores. Now, however, retailers recognize the advantages—for maximizing profitability per square metre and improving stock control—of linking their computerized inventory management systems to the sales order systems of their suppliers. Facings and promotional activity are important influences on the store level movement of goods. Suppliers' representatives, by visiting stores and collecting information via portable computer links, can provide an almost instant analysis of recent sales at store level. Companies who have yet to introduce such technology into their salesforce and order entry operations may soon find difficulty in working with intermediaries who demand this level of cooperation.[7]

SUPPLIERS

Marketeers who focus their attention on market trends and competition may overlook the threats and opportunities created by changes in the supply situation. This myopic perspective is based on an assumption among some marketeers that the procurement/manufacturing group should manage all aspects of the supply situation. A classic example of the threat posed by a change in supply was that of the plastics industry during the OPEC oil crisis in the mid-seventies. Despite the fact that the potential implications of an OPEC cartel had been predicted several years earlier, marketeers in the industry had made little attempt to develop contingency plans to accommodate the impact of a shortage in feedstocks and rapidly rising raw material prices. Most marketing strategies were based upon exploiting the benefits of large-scale manufacturing operations to supply high-volume/low-unit price market conditions. As the OPEC oil embargo constricted feedstock supplies, companies were forced to cut back production to levels well below break-even, and without any alternative plans to exploit lower volume/higher quality segments, some companies were forced to close their manufacturing plants.

As illustrated in Fig. 2.4, the influence of supply on future marketing activities is not merely limited to physical shortages in raw materials. Attitude shifts among suppliers can also create problems: for example, an overseas supplier withdrawing from the market for political reasons; the financial community deciding that another industrial sector provides a lower risk/higher return investment proposition.

Companies are also placed at risk if marketing plans do not include the influence that new entrants or changes in technology may have on the supply situation. This is especially vital if these changes can be used as an opportunity for a competitor to gain an advantage over the company's current market position (e.g., those car manufacturers who ignored the benefits of using suppliers of production systems that incorporated robotics

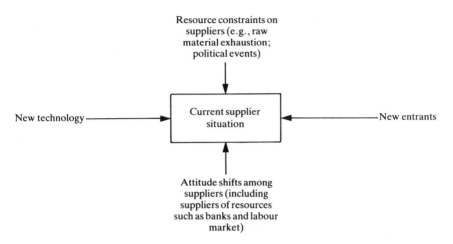

Figure 2.4 Forces of change in the supply base situation.

to improve product quality and/or reduce production costs; steel producers who have not moved from open hearth to electric and oxygen furnace technology to improve unit costs). Given the potential benefits in cost and quality that can be provided by existing suppliers through new technology or new entrants to the supply scene, it is therefore imperative that marketeers develop much closer links with procurement/manufacturing departments in order to incorporate such opportunities into future marketing plans.

This perspective is most important for companies in mature markets where survival is often dependent upon sustaining quality while concurrently holding or reducing costs.[8] One of the reasons that the Japanese have successfully entered a number of world markets on a quality/reasonable price platform has been due in part to their ability to exploit the benefits of close working links between their marketing, manufacturing and R&D operations. Yet many marketing personnel in the UK still ignore the opportunities that can exist through working more closely with the supply side of the business management equation.

ENVIRONMENTAL TURBULENCE

Many companies are finding it increasingly difficult to predict, with any accuracy, the future market conditions.[9] A common source of this environmental turbulence is change in the macroenvironment surrounding the core market system. Such changes often have an impact on a number of elements within the core system. An example is the advent of perestroika, which could have a number of consequences, including:

- the opening up of new markets in Eastern bloc countries for computer manufacturers;
- communist countries being permitted to expand production of consumer goods which compete with EC producers in their own home markets;
- a decline in defence industry sales following adoption of an arms reduction policy by NATO countries.

Some marketeers do not manage to develop an adequate understanding of the influence of the macroenvironment on core systems. But even for those marketeers who have acquired this broader perspective, there are a number of factors that may impair their ability to interpret forecasted changes in environmental conditions.

(a) The variable may be in an area outside the understanding of the observer (e.g., attempting to comprehend the application of superconductivity on the home computer market).
(b) Early information may be vague and difficult to interpret (e.g., signs of an attitude shift in a small number of the European consumer population about pollution in the early eighties, which has led to a large new market opportunity for environmentally safe products).
(c) The ultimate financial impact on the company of potential increases in operating costs cannot yet be estimated (e.g., the reduction of smoke emissions from factories in order to conform to new laws designed to eliminate the acid rain problem in Europe).
(d) The possibility that two or more minor changes in the macroenvironment may interact in an unpredictable way (e.g., the outcome of these three factors—(1) expanding market for leisure craft in the UK, (2) redirection of policing efforts to manage inner city violence, and (3) rising labour costs for security guards—was a rapid growth in remote video-monitoring systems for marinas in the UK).

Given the complex interaction of variables within the business environment, some companies have now accepted that the mere extrapolation of past events is not a sufficiently sound basis upon which to develop future marketing strategies. One technique available to marketeers in such companies is 'scenario planning'. This involves making alternative assumptions about a range of variables in the business environment and combining these to create pictures or scenarios about the future. Such scenarios may identify more clearly the key factors that might influence both industry and corporate level future performance.[10]

In order to stimulate proactive marketing plans a number of scenarios can be examined which cover the entire spectrum of possible conditions the company could face over the next few years. To ensure the scenarios are a complete representation of all aspects of the business environment, it is recommended that the marketeer involves staff from other departments in the process of defining possible changes in important variables. Where there is a risk that internal cross-organizational analysis will be biased towards firmly entrenched corporate opinions, the marketing department may wish to involve specialists from outside including scientists, politicians, economists, and other members of the market system such as representation from key suppliers.

The rapidly declining cost of free standing and networked personal computers has caused a resurgence of interest in the benefits of creating management information systems (MIS). These can hold a number of data bases that can be used to ask 'what if' questions about future performance. Attempts have been made to integrate the MIS approach into scenario planning. Unfortunately, many key variables in the scenarios are of a qualitative nature. Hence, although the MIS approach to planning is a powerful tool, the marketeer is urged to avoid those ardent disciples of operations research (OR) who insist on restricting evaluation to those variables that can be modelled on a computer using multivariate predictive equations.[11]

MANAGING INFORMATION

The complexity of the business environment and the availability of information are both increasing at an exponential rate. In response to this situation, some marketing departments may restrict their analysis to variables that they consider of immediate relevance to near-future performance. Although marketeers should have accumulated a wealth of information during the process of managing the company/market interface, their knowledge may in fact be very limited. When other departments in the organization are unable to obtain required information from this source, they may create their own data bases and use these for their planning activities. This situation is most noticeable in research and development groups who often find it more practical to progress work on new technologies and only involve the marketing group when product commercialization seems feasible.[12]

If marketeers are to continue to justify their position as a centre of expertise on future events, they must create and sustain a comprehensive data collection and analysis capability within their group. Furthermore, if they wish to be perceived as contributing to an integrated approach to organizational management, they must actively involve other departments in the acquisition and evaluation of information on all aspects of the business environment. One way to fulfil this objective is to link the marketing department data bases into organizational data files and create cross-organizational discussion groups which are administered by the marketing department. An important part of the assumed responsibility is to circulate summaries of such meetings to interested parties throughout the company.

There should also be a willingness to utilize marketing department budgets to support multidisciplinary investigations of issues that may have major potential influence on corporate performance. For those marketeers who are concerned about diverting funds away from what they perceive as purely marketing issues, it is worth remembering that 'knowledge is power'.

REFERENCES

1. T. Levitt, 'Marketing myopia', *Harvard Business Review*, July 1960.
2. W. R. Smith, 'Product differentiation and market segmentation marketing strategies', *Journal of Marketing*, July 1956.
3. J. G. Myers, S. A. Greyser and W. F. Massy, 'The effectiveness of marketing's R&D for marketing management: an assessment', *Journal of Marketing*, vol. 43, pp. 17–29, 1979.
4. F. C. Alexander, 'Is industrial marketing ready to go consumer?', *Industrial Marketing*, December 1964.
5. A. C. Cooper and D. Schendel, 'Strategic response to technological threats', *Business Horizons*, February 1976.
6. M. E. Porter, *Competitive Strategy Techniques for Analysing Industries and Competition*, Free Press, 1980.
7. T. Peters, *Thriving on Chaos*, Macmillan, 1987.
8. W. K. Hall, 'Survival strategies in a hostile environment', *Harvard Business Review*, September 1980.
9. H. I. Ansoff, *Implanting Strategic Management*, Prentice-Hall, 1984.
10. S. C. Wheelwright and E. A. Makridakis, *Forecasting Methods for Management*, Wiley, 1980.
11. J. S. Baylis, *Marketing for Engineers: IEE Management of Technology*, vol. 4, 1985.
12. J. J. Verschurr, *Technology and Markets: IEE Management of Technology*, vol. 1, 1983.

THREE

INTERNAL CAPABILITY AND VULNERABILITY

FUNCTIONAL INTERRELATIONSHIPS

Although recognizing the non-scientific nature of the sample frame, the author's personal experience of marketeers is that they usually appear to be enthusiastic optimists who assume that, having set an objective, it can be achieved. This contrasts with the comparable experience of managers from other functional disciplines who have a technological, scientific or financial background. They appear to assess more carefully whether their department or they have the necessary capability to carry out a task before undertaking to meet a stated objective. Although the marketeers' ability to exhibit eternal hope is a useful personal attribute, it is possibly not the best basis upon which to run a successful business.

All marketeers must comprehend the need to assess internal organizational weaknesses that might be an obstacle to the successful execution of new plans and policies. Equally, they must not assume that because an objective is important, resources can always be found to overcome any operational problem. This is most likely to occur in companies where the marketing department is a dominant influence, because other departmental managers may be wary of expressing concerns about their own resource capability in case this is interpreted as being obstructive.

A few years ago, when the business environment was less competitive, marketeers could probably have ignored the possible risk of inadequate internal capability. In those days companies usually had time to learn from their mistakes and retroactively remedied problems in the marketplace as these became apparent. Competitors are now more alert to any signs of

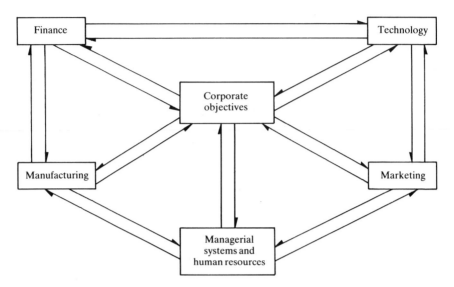

Figure 3.1 Functional elements within the corporate system.

weakness, however, because this can be a leverage point through which to block new marketing initiatives. The marketeer must therefore recognize that new or revised plans should only be implemented if they do not exacerbate areas in which the company is vulnerable to competitive response.

Given the functional interactions shown in Fig. 3.1, it is apparent that the marketeer cannot restrict analysis of capability to his own department, but will have to extend the assessment across other areas of the organization. A planning concept which has become very popular in recent years is SWOT (Strengths, Weaknesses, Opportunities and Threats analysis). This mechanism helps managers to focus on the internal capabilities of the organization and to relate these conclusions to the business environment in which the company operates. The recommended application of the SWOT technique is to exploit areas of corporate strength by matching these to business opportunities. What seems to be forgotten is the principle that 'a chain is only as strong as its weakest link'. It is therefore suggested that the marketeer will have to reach an understanding of areas of corporate weakness, because in the short term it is preferable to develop plans that protect these from additional external pressures. Over the longer term, the marketeer can then work with other managers to remove these areas of vulnerability, for it is only after this has been achieved that the company will be in a strong enough position to successfully implement a more aggressive, growth-orientated strategy.

MARKETING CAPABILITY

A key role of the marketeer is the ability to use the '4 Ps' in the marketing mix—product, price, promotion and place (i.e., distribution)—to optimize corporate performance.[1] Weaknesses within the mix will create difficulties in even sustaining current sales levels unless other companies also face similar problems. Any attempts to generate incremental sales, however, are very likely to fail. Furthermore, in certain circumstances, expansionist actions by the marketing department could drive the company to the brink of financial disaster. The probability of this latter outcome will be even higher in those market sectors where one element of the mix is a dominant influence in determining customer purchase decisions.

PRODUCT AS A DOMINANT FACTOR

In certain market sectors undergoing rapid technological change, a company's success will rest on its ability to continually supply goods that are tangibly superior in performance to those offered by competitors.[2] One example of this is the machine tool industry which supplies production equipment to manufacturing companies. Customers for machine tools need to sustain quality and cost stability in their manufacturing operations. Hence, in the machine tool market there is increasing demand for the application of (a) computer numerical control (CNC) technology to reduce set-up times and increase production flexibility and (b) integration of computer-aided design (CAD) with computer-aided manufacturing systems (CAM). The marketing department of a machine tool company would be unable to deliver a sales growth strategy if certain weaknesses were evident; for example, if

- products were rated as average to poor in the utilization of new computer technologies;
- products were perceived as being technically obsolete;
- products were unreliable and/or training or repair services were poor after sales installation;
- introductions of new product were limited to launching duplicates of concepts already marketed by competitors.

PRICE AS A DOMINANT FACTOR

Where there is minimal opportunity for companies to provide products with noticeable differences in performance and major economies of scale are available in extraction and/or processing, then price is often the dominant factor in the customer's decision to purchase. These conditions are found in many primary producer commodity markets such as agriculture, fishing and mineral extraction. In these industries, a marketing plan to expand sales would weaken the corporate position if one or more of the following were characteristics of the company's operations:

- The company has a relatively small production operation and is unable to exploit any economy of scale opportunities.
- Production costs are similar to the actual prices quoted by competitors who operate reasonably profitable operations.
- There are inadequate financial reserves to support any response to heavy price discounting by competitors during periods of supply/demand imbalance.
- The company has been unable to establish a price leadership position and is always forced to postpone any price actions until after moves by the majority of competitors.

An example of pure competition causing the closure of smaller companies was the collapse of the World Tin Council in the early eighties. This organization had been created to stabilize world tin prices by holding stocks in periods of supply/demand imbalance; when the Council was unable to continue in its role, prices fell dramatically. The UK tin-mining industry is based upon a number of small-scale operations in Cornwall. These companies operate deep mines and extraction costs are extremely high. Elsewhere in the world tin ore can be obtained through lower cost open-cast mining technology, so these operations were able to survive because production costs were near to the market price for the ore. Operating costs for Cornish mines were much higher than the new price for ore, and hence many companies were forced to close down.

PROMOTION AS A DOMINANT FACTOR

Product technology in some market sectors may not provide the basis for more than minor performance differences between products, but high unit profitability will support heavy promotional activity through which to create perceived differences between competitive offerings. This situation is found in many consumer non-durable markets such as detergents, soft drinks and toiletries. A company attempting to increase its market share under these conditions would encounter problems if it had:

- a weak, poorly trained salesforce;
- a low promotional expenditure/sales ratio compared to major competitors;
- promotional funds that were restricted by low sales base and/or profit margin relative to other companies in the same industry;

- a low awareness by consumers of company's benefit claim in the market;
- products that were not perceived as differentiated from other brands;
- product benefit claims of a type that meant the company was unable to respond effectively to a competitor's change in promotional campaign;
- sales promotions that had little impact on customer purchase behaviour;
- sales promotions that were rarely supported by intermediaries;
- an overall corporate image that was either weak or non-existent among final customers and/or intermediaries.

There is little real tangible difference between the lending, saving and money transaction products offered by institutions in the consumer financial services market. Until recently, the UK building societies were restricted by law to offering a very limited range of 'money products'. Removal of these restrictions by the government has been followed by a rapid expansion of the product portfolios of the large national societies. To build customer awareness and market share, these organizations have used television advertising campaigns on a scale not previously seen in this market sector. Given the relatively low profit margin in providing consumer financial services, these campaigns are only made affordable if the company has a high market share. The regional societies in the UK have a much smaller customer base and cannot afford to compete in a promotional spending battle with the national organizations. Hence, in a market where promotional spending has become the dominant factor, the smaller societies are looking towards repositioning themselves as providers in specific, specialist customer-need market niches in order to survive.

PLACE AS A DOMINANT FACTOR

If the requirement is for a standard, undifferentiated product, the demand is somewhat volatile, the customer can buy from more than one source, and the supplier company is responsible for managing delivery, then sales volume will be heavily influenced by a company's distribution management capability. This situation is found in sectors supplying certain fresh foods (e.g., meat, vegetables and fruit) and manufacturers of standard specification industrial components whose Original Equipment Manufacturers (OEM) customers are using a 'just in time' (JIT) manufacturing philosophy.[3] A company attempting to increase sales in this type of market is inviting disaster if certain weaknesses are evident in their operation; that is, if they are:

- forced to use unreliable contract shippers to deliver product;
- operating an order entry system that cannot rapidly match stocks to customer requirements;
- unable to hold buffer stocks to handle sudden increases in demand;

- almost incapable of meeting agreed delivery schedules;
- incapable of responding rapidly to quality problems or changes in product specification from customers and still meet delivery dates.

A characteristic of some industries is that the intermediary has a critical role in the linking of companies to customers. In this case, the company obviously must ensure that its intermediary does not exhibit the above weaknesses. An example of this situation is to be found in the automobile industry where a manufacturer could launch a technically superior new car which would fail in the marketplace because the distributor network contains a significant proportion of incompetent dealers.[4]

FINANCIAL CAPABILITY

Most marketeers are attracted by any proposition that offers further growth in absolute sales or profitability. It is rarely the case that their assessment of an opportunity is extended to encompass the impact on (a) the company's working capital position or (b) the ability to raise external funds to support future capital investment plans.

This orientation towards sales/profitability parameters among many marketeers has possibly been caused by their early training with large national or multinational companies. Such organizations tend to have adequate cash reserves and a financial track record which allows them to borrow from external sources such as banks or the stock market. In addition, corporate accountants can compound this problem by their tendency to believe that management of the balance sheet is their special preserve. In these circumstances they will not actively seek marketing department involvement in decisions to optimize asset balances, other than to complain about customers who have caused unnecessary increases in the level or average age of the accounts receivables.

Smaller companies are often in a less secure financial position.[5] Here, marketeers really do need to examine the potential impact of short-term actions which, although they might generate incremental revenue, may concurrently create balance sheet problems that could obstruct implementation of longer term business strategies. This concept can be illustrated by the disguised case of Orion Ltd. This company manufactures vehicle spares and components. Output is sold under the Orion label to independent garages and as an own-label product to national chain DIY outlets. In recent years the company has faced intense price competition from overseas competitors and this has severely depressed financial performance (Table 3.1). Recently, however, the company has acquired the European licensing rights to innovative technology that would permit them to launch a low-cost, electronic diagnostic engine emission and tuning system. A UK sub-

Table 3.1 Financial performance and forecast of impact on adding new retailer

Profit and loss accounts (£'000)

	Three years ago	Current year	Forecast
Sales	776	700	800
Cost of goods	577	533	622
Gross profit	199	167	178
Other expenses	117.6	124	126
Net profit	81.4	43	52
(Profit as % sales)	(10.5)	(6.1)	(6.5)

Balance sheet £'000)

	Three years ago	Current year	Forecast
Fixed assets			
(net of depreciation)	220	170	162
Current assets			
Finished goods/			
work-in-progress	174	170	204
Debtors	160	156	226
Total current assets	334	326	430
Liabilities due in			
less than 12 months			
Creditors	126	123	125
Overdraft	90	100	186
Total	216	223	311
Net current assets	118	103	119
Liabilities due in			
less than 12 months	75	70	68
Capital employed	263	203	213

contractor has been located to manufacture the equipment and Orion will have to invest £100 000 over the next nine months to fund the product launch. Their recent financial performance has caused some difficulty in obtaining incremental external funds, but a merchant bank has now agreed to provide support in return for a minority equity share in the company.

In the meantime the marketing department has been actively seeking new outlets for the company's existing products, and has located a large DIY chain whose primary supplier cannot meet the retailer's needs during the peak winter sales period. It is estimated that this new source of business will generate £100 000 in additional sales at a gross profit margin of 18 per cent. The marketing director has, therefore, recommended that Orion exploit this new source of business on the grounds that it will increase both sales and net profits.

Fortunately the finance director suspects that the new customer may place additional financial burdens on the company because Orion will be expected to carry adequate finished goods ('buffer stocks') to meet any unexpected sales increases in the customer's retail outlets. Furthermore, as Orion is only a secondary supplier, it is likely that the retailer will delay payment on outstanding Orion invoices whenever possible. The finance director has therefore prepared a new forecast based upon his pessimistic opinions about the likely behaviour of the customer. The results in Table 3.1 show that although sales and profits will rise, this will be accompanied by an increase in the level of both debtor and finished goods balances. The only source of funds to support such an increase in current assets would be through borrowing on overdraft from a bank.

The resultant current asset/liability position would probably not be viewed favourably by the merchant bankers who are prepared to support the new product project. So the finance director has persuaded the marketing department to reconsider acceptance of this new source of business, on the grounds that an inability to raise additional venture capital could possibly halt the proposed investment programme designed to place Orion in a more competitive position over the longer term.

Even where a company's balance sheet is in a much healthier position than the Orion example, marketeers must be certain that resources are sufficient to defend the company in the face of a threat from competitors. The world of business is littered with the battered shells of companies who identified an unfilled or growth market opportunity that they exploited ahead of larger, less perceptive national operations. Then, instead of pausing to consolidate their initial success, these small companies aggressively moved to increase their market share still further. At this point the 'Goliaths' in the industry could no longer ignore the new 'David' and their heavy promotional retaliation or price-cutting activities either destroyed or severely weakened the smaller company. An example of this situation is Laker Airlines who challenged the larger carriers by offering cut price Atlantic airfares. In the end the weight of response by large European and American carriers was one of the factors that forced this brave challenger into bankruptcy.

Estimating the financial resources to defend market position is even more difficult for companies who are using a new technology to create or expand a new market. In the early years there are no accurate data on sales potential, so the company cannot predict whether the potential sales volume will ever be of a size to attract competitive response from large companies not yet active in the market. In such cases, management is often split on whether to invest funds in accelerating product development or in building reserves to support an adequate defence at a later date.[6] Realistically, if the market does become very attractive the larger organizations will eventually move in and take over. Possibly, therefore, the best decision for the smaller firm is to invest in capturing the largest possible sales base, on the grounds that a strong market position will increase the price a large competitor is willing to pay to acquire the operation. An example of this type of situation is the market for industrial lasers where, in the early years, product application pioneering was carried out by a number of small, specialist companies. Once the larger firms recognized the true market potential, they moved to purchase existing operations as the fastest route to gaining management expertise in this area of technology. Those companies that resisted takeover bids and chose to remain independent are now finding the cost of defending their business extremely high.·

MANUFACTURING CAPABILITY

Most marketing tasks can be executed over a short time span and without any significant investment in capital assets. This experience is probably an important factor in the failure by some marketeers to balance the viability of marketing plans against the company's manufacturing capability. Marketeers may assume that having determined the quality, cost and quantity parameters defined by the customer, the fulfilling of these specifications should be a relatively simple task for the production department.

In the west over the last thirty years, the marketeers' disregard for working with the manufacturing group to optimize output seems to have increased. Analysis of many Japanese successes has revealed that competitive advantage is based upon a careful matching of market opportunity to production capability.[7] It should be an obvious fact that marketing plans that are incompatible with manufacturing capability will eventually place the company in a vulnerable position.

Manufacturing systems have usually evolved over a number of years as the company has selected the most appropriate system to optimize the balance between supply and demand. If the company has created a low-volume batch production system to meet extreme product specification variations across the customer base, then it is not likely to be able to compete on unit cost basis with organizations who have established higher volume, product-focused plant systems. Hence the marketing department would be ill-advised to attempt to implement a plan to expand into the market sector for standardized, uniform products. For example, a company originally established to produce circuit boards for specialist applications should not attempt to enter the market sector of supplying standard circuit boards for a multinational consumer electrical goods manufacturer. And the reverse also applies: a high-volume producer would be vulnerable if the new marketing plan moved the company towards supplying small volume runs of customized product.[8]

Another issue that must be considered is the age of the production system. It is sometimes the case that the company is operating old, fully depreciated capital assets. Fixed overheads will be a minor element in the cost of goods and the company's low operating costs in a price-sensitive sector in the market is the reason it is successful. The marketing department would be unwise to assume that these costs will remain unchanged and attempt to expand sales while holding price at current levels. At the point where replacement machinery has to be acquired to handle increased demand, fixed overheads will rise dramatically and the company will move to a much less competitive position. If this replacement equipment involves new technologies because other companies have already adopted these systems to sustain productivity, the company will also have to cope with a period of higher than normal operating costs while production operatives learn to use the new machines.

TECHNOLOGICAL CAPABILITY

Over recent years, companies have relied upon technology-based innovations to sustain their current market position and to exploit new areas of opportunity. It has been suggested[9] that technology can be classified into three specific types:

1. Pacer technology, which could permit a company to completely overturn the current market situation (e.g., a 'stealth' jet fighter).
2. Key technology, which is the leading edge of existing technology and will permit a company to remain ahead of competition (e.g., IBM's 360 Computer System).
3. Base technology, which is the minimal technology a company requires in order to remain an effective member of an industry.

When considering new strategies, it is imperative that the marketeer comprehends the capability of the company in managing the development and introduction of new technology. There is little point, for example, in a plan to move ahead of competition with new products that are based on major technological innovation if the company is only competent in managing the industry's base technology.

The importance of technology will vary across different markets and industries. In certain sectors, technology is both stable and long-lived with product-based competition centring on improving design features or introducing minor reformulations (e.g., many non-durable consumer goods). In this environment marketeers will be able to sustain a reasonable rate of new product introductions even if the company has minimal R&D expertise (e.g., the launch of liquid detergents for washing machines in the UK). In some industries the base technology may be sufficiently fertile to provide constant opportunities to update products by offering progressive improvements in performance or new applications (e.g., new generations of penicillin-based drugs in the pharmaceutical industry).

Marketeers operating in fertile technology industries will face major constraints if the company has a weak R&D capability. Some areas of technology are so fertile that products are continually being rendered obsolete by innovations (e.g., computer software). Companies that survive in this environment are wholly dependent upon sustained reinvestment in R&D. Leading edge technology has provided the opportunity to spawn new highly successful businesses that are often able to enter markets previously dominated by large multinationals. The owners of these new entrant operations are usually technologists with no marketing expertise.[6] As the company expands, the new marketing staff may discover that the company lacks the R&D capability to develop second- or third-generation products successfully. New product strategies will have to be restricted to short-term concepts that will only extend the life of existing products by a few years (e.g., some of the smaller companies who have entered the personal computer market). Beyond this point, such companies may enter a decline phase unless acquired by larger organizations who have the resources to support major new R&D programmes (e.g., Olivetti's acquisition of the UK computer manufacturer Acorn in the early eighties).

MANAGERIAL CAPABILITY

Ultimately the success or failure of any business will depend upon the ability of the management team. They will be required to assess situations, review available information and reach decisions. How well these processes are executed is dependent upon the behaviour or managerial style of the organization.[10]

Marketeers are sometimes so certain of the validity of their recommendations that they forget that, in order to be accepted and implemented, the proposal must be compatible with the managerial values of the organization. In industries where the business environment has been extremely stable, management behaviour will tend to have evolved towards optimizing internal efficiency. This will be reflected by information systems which focus on precise measurements of internal activity and emphasize forecasting approaches based upon extrapolation of past trends. Departments will tend to be inward looking, seeking to improve their performance relative to the standards as specified by the control system. There will be little motivation to integrate activities with other areas of the organization, and departments will endeavour to protect their current span of responsibilities. In this type of environment, a marketeer who proposes a new plan based upon inspired visions of future opportunities—especially if these place the company in a high-risk situation and involve major departmental restructuring—will encounter severe opposition to any proposals. Furthermore, even when a plan has been accepted, resistance to change and little experience of interdepartmental integration will probably combine to create major errors during the implementation phase of the new plan.

An example of the above scenario is provided by Andrew Lamb, a marketing adviser to City of London merchant banks, who, in commenting on why marketing has yet to get off the ground, stated that:

> Generally speaking, investment bankers are very poor at planned communications. Their entrepreneurial culture tends to be antipathetic, with each department concerned principally with its own bottom line. Marketing is seen as a front-line preserve, particularly among dealers whose time-frame may be more than a few seconds. Historically the bank's evolution is shaped by its corporate finance department, which is regarded by itself as the bank's soul. Banks were loose-knit federations of entrepreneurs, whose boards were effectively descendants from the days when they were partnerships. Business development is dictated by financially driven operating plans and budgets whose primary driving force is cash division's profit expectations.

Companies operating in a more volatile industrial sector often survive by adopting a more entrepreneurial business style. Managers are interested in trying new approaches that involve creative solutions based upon little or no accurate market information. Departments are enthusiastic about sharing opinions and actively seek mechanisms to integrate their areas of activity with other groups across the organization. Confronted with new problems, staff are eager to examine the widest possible range of alternative actions, even to the point of executing parallel solutions as a possible method of finding the optimal future approach.[11]

This environment may seem very exciting to the newly recruited marketeer who has previously worked in a more conservative organization. If the company is then found to be operating in a market sector that is moving towards maturity, the corporate culture could now be inappropriate. In a mature market, where new sales can only come from share gains from competition, the company's future will depend upon becoming more efficient and controlled. Unless senior management are willing to accept the need for a more controlled approach the marketeer may have difficulty gaining acceptance of moves to a more disciplined style of marketing. The company may reject the new conservatism altogether and elect to remain an entrepreneurial operation, which could then necessitate a move into new markets or technologies. The marketeer should, therefore, make a careful assessment of the managerial capabilities required before taking the company into areas where few personnel have any real expertise.

REFERENCES

1. E. J. McCarthy, *Basic Marketing: A Managerial Approach*, 4th edn, Irwin, 1971.
2. C. G. Ryan, *The Marketing of Technology: IEE Management of Technology* vol. 3, 1984.
3. D. A. Garvin, *Managing Quality*, Free Press, 1988.

4. B. Mayon-White, *Planning and Managing Change*, The Open University, 1986.
5. R. T. Davis and G. Smith, *Marketing in Emerging Companies*, Addison Wesley, 1984.
6. R. F. Hartley, *Marketing Mistakes*, 3rd edn, Wiley, 1986.
7. R. T. Pascale and A. G. Athos, *The Art of Japanese Management*, Penguin, 1982.
8. R. R. Rothberg, *Corporate Strategy and Product Innovation*, 2nd edn, Free Press, 1981.
9. R. B. Lamb, *Competitive Strategic Management*, Prentice-Hall, 1984.
10. D. Robey, *Designing Organisations*, 2nd edn, Irwin, 1985.
11. T. Morse, 'Banking: stony ground for creative growth', *Marketing Week*, pp. 46–51, 24 June 1988.

FOUR

SELECTING APPROPRIATE STRATEGIES

MARKET LEADERSHIP

The on-going battle for market share between companies such as Pepsi versus Coca-Cola, Nestlé versus General Foods, Boeing versus Airbus Industries and Motorola versus Intel, is evidence that market leadership is a popular strategy among marketeers. The accepted benefit of the strategy is that absolute profitability can be maximized by exploiting the economies of scale available to whichever organization supplies the majority of market demand. Leadership also has a personal appeal because marketeers have long understood the value to their own careers of involvement in the management of a nationally or internationally recognized product leader.

Major companies are not just interested in absolute profits but also seek to optimize the level of profits generated on assets employed (i.e., return on investment or return on capital employed). Hence marketeers were gratified to learn of the profit impact of management strategies (PIMS) study in the early seventies, which concluded that ROI rises linearly with market share.[1, 2] This research demonstrated that businesses with market shares in excess of 40 per cent had an average ROI of 30 per cent, whereas companies with a market share of less than 10 per cent would normally only achieve an ROI of 7–10 per cent.

The PIMS project has been widely utilized by the marketing profession to justify their viewpoint that market leadership is the most suitable strategy for a successful company. Furthermore, the PIMS data have proved very useful when a marketeer is seeking approval for further increases in marketing budgets to support heavier weight advertising campaigns or sales promotion programmes. It is not possible to assess the number of companies that have been damaged by marketeers who have blindly applied the formula

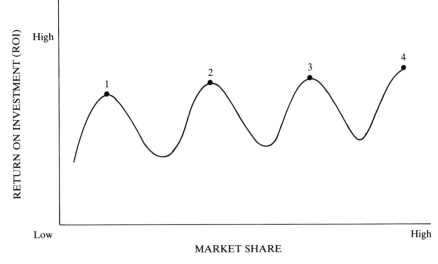

Figure 4.1 Relationship between scale of operation/market position and ROI.

that expenditure to build share in mature markets will always be beneficial; but it does not seem unreasonable to suggest that the financial failure of some businesses in recent years can in part be attributed to unsuccessful attempts by marketeers to elevate their companies towards a higher share of the market.

Research subsequent to the PIMS study has found numerous examples of companies with a low market share, but an ROI similar or equal to that of market leaders.[3] The usual explanation for this phenomenon is that the smaller companies have chosen to concentrate on a specific market sector to avoid the very expensive proposition of a head-on confrontation with market leaders. By specializing in this way, such companies are able to optimize their scale of internal business functions such as marketing, production and distribution to match the requirements of their limited customer base.

It is quite possible that, in many industries, two or more peaks in ROI may exist relative to market share. As suggested by Fig. 4.1, the peaks might exist at:

- Position 1—a small regional company.
- Position 2—a national company which operates in a specialist market sector.
- Position 3—the traditional, mass market national market leader.
- Position 4—a multinational organization that has achieved market leadership on a global scale.

Companies which find themselves in a position on the downside of the curve beyond points 1, 2 or 3 in Fig. 4.1 may actually risk a decline in ROI if they implement a strategy of seeking a higher market share. In fact, such companies might benefit from executing a reverse growth strategy because some reduction in size would significantly improve ROI. Unfortunately, it is a rare marketeer who can turn down the exciting prospect of working with larger promotional budgets and/or the opportunity to expand the scale of operations within the marketing department.

The leadership concept has its roots in the market conditions of the late nineteenth and early twentieth century when most customers sought to purchase the same basic commodities. These homogeneous demand conditions led to the creation of large-scale manufacturing facilities capable of generating output at a very low unit cost. In such situations the prime role of the marketing group would be to initiate promotional schemes that sustained a high level of sales and thereby ensured company plants were operating near to 100 per cent of capacity.

In an increasingly affluent society customers are likely to be able to afford a more diverse range of products. In these circumstances, companies that operate a strategy of offering a single, standard product at the lowest possible price as a route to market leadership face two possible risks. First, a more 'market aware' competitor may make available a range of products which more effectively fulfils customer needs. After the First World War, Henry Ford built his empire on a uniform product and is remembered for his famous promise that customers could have any colour they wanted as long as it was black. General Motors correctly identified the market trend towards a desire for a greater choice in car models and, by making these available, took a significant proportion of market share away from the Ford Company.

The second risk of cost-based leadership is a downturn in market demand. If a company has built business through intense price competition made possible by economies of scale in the manufacturing operation, then as market size decreases the company will be placed in the position of owning capacity in excess of demand. The company may be forced to enter into even greater price competition to generate the sales needed merely to absorb the fixed costs associated with ownership of large production facilities. If market demand does not improve the company may go bankrupt, because it can no longer generate profit sufficient even to meet the interest charges on the debts accumulated while selling products at below cost. This type of situation has been very common over the last ten years in basic industries such as steel, mining and shipbuilding. While some of the large companies that had based their market position on cost-based price competition were forced out of business, those companies that had established a market position of offering specialist, high-quality products were often able to survive, and in some cases actually increased market share (e.g., the large shipyards on Tyneside in the north-east of England versus a specialist yard such as that at Appledore in north Devon).

SEGMENTATION STRATEGIES

Recognition of the benefits of servicing a small specialist market niche in zero growth mature markets has caused some companies to favour 'market segmentation' over leadership as a more viable corporate strategy. Initially companies used relatively simple concepts such as demographics or geography as the basis for isolating segment opportunities. As more sophisticated market research tools have become available, however, new approaches to segmentation involving techniques such as psychographics and buyer behaviour modelling have been introduced.[4]

It is necessary to accept, however, that by servicing the needs of a specific customer group, total potential sales revenue is much lower than it would be if the company offered items with a broad range of appeal across the entire market. Given the more limited sales potential within a market segment, a company needs to analyse carefully the total costs of formulating and launching a new, specialist product.[5] Without a very detailed study of both market demand and actual costs of production, one of two outcomes may occur (as shown in Fig. 4.2*a*):

- Case 1 where, upon introduction of the new product, the segment is found to contain insufficient customers who actually adopt the product.
- Case 2 where a high unit demand is only achieved at very low prices and, hence, the sector is only marginally profitable.

Even after a company has successfully entered a new segment, the marketeer must carefully assess any new proposition that might erode the differential between costs and revenue. A standard technique in mass marketing is to consolidate the market position further by the introduction of product line extensions. However, within a specialist market segment the total potential sales are often very limited. If this is the case, as shown in Fig. 4.2*b*, the introduction of line extension items may only cause a minor increase in total consumption. It is likely that total operating costs will have risen, making the subsequent net profit position poorer than that which existed prior to the launch of the new products.

The other important factor to be considered in adopting a segmentation strategy is whether the segments will remain of an adequate size during periods of economic recession. In the late seventies a number of companies in the leisure boat industry found that, as the total market shrank in response to the world recession, a number of segments virtually disappeared because few buyers were willing to risk any outlay on specialist customized boats. Those companies who had built their business around one narrow segment could not sustain sales, whereas competitors who operated across a number of market niches were able to generate sufficient sales to survive until the market conditions began to improve in 1982/3.

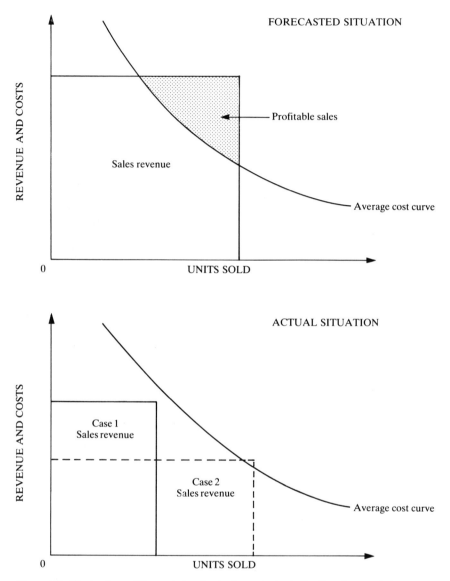

Figure 4.2a Comparison of forecasted and actual revenue/cost situations in a market segment.

PRODUCT PORTFOLIO STRATEGIES

Despite some criticism of the concept,[6] it is widely accepted that the life of most products will pass through the four stages[7] of introduction, growth, maturity and decline shown in Fig. 4.3. The concept, which is known as the 'product lifecycle' (PLC), has important implications for corporate

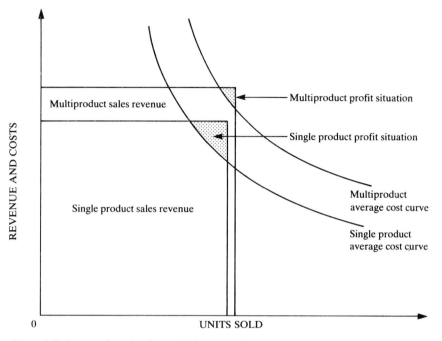

Figure 4.2*b* Impact of moving from a single to a multiproduct position within a market segment.

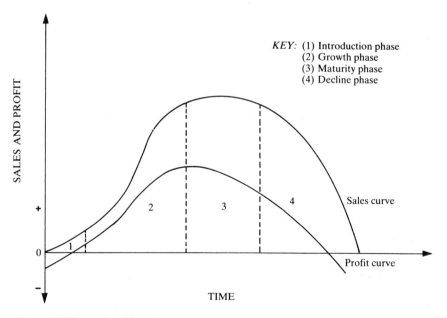

Figure 4.3 The product lifecycle.

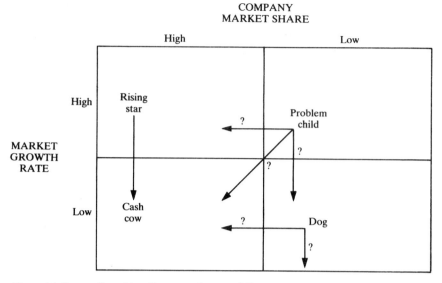

Figure 4.4 Boston Consulting Group product portfolio concept.

profitability.[8] During the introduction phase sales are low, promotional expenditure to generate trial is high and profits are minimal. In the growth phase, more customers are trying the product and some are becoming regular users, so profits rise. During maturity, the main source of additional sales is by attracting customers from other companies. As the level of competition intensifies, profits begin to fall. Ultimately a product will move into the decline phase and the company will start losing money unless the product is discontinued.

In today's increasingly competitive environment, the length of time between introduction and the onset of decline is becoming shorter. Furthermore, as more companies have become skilled at defending their business, it is increasingly difficult for new companies to enter a market successfully after the product lifecycle has moved into the maturity phase.

The Boston Consulting Group (BCG) encapsulated application of the PLC concept in their product share/market status decision model matrix (Fig. 4.4) by suggesting that successful companies need at least two products in their strategic portfolio.[9] One product should have a high share in a mature market. The revenue from this product or 'cash cow' can then be used to fund the introduction of a successful new product (the 'rising star') which is destined to be 'tomorrow's cash cow'. This elegantly simple model has been very useful in marketeers' horizons beyond that of focusing all resources in the attempt to achieve or retain market leadership during the mature market phase.

Products that have a low market share in a mature market are labelled by the model as 'dogs' to communicate graphically that efforts to attract market share from larger companies is usually a misuse of corporate resources. A similar question mark hangs over new products that have only achieved a low share. These are known as 'problem children' because they will probably evolve into a 'dog' as the market matures.

A major risk in applying the model is to assume that high market share, as with the earlier PIMS concept, is the only route to corporate success.[10] Absolute acceptance of the Boston Consulting Group model could result in companies wishing to operate only in markets where they can be a dominant force, and withdrawing from any sector where only a small market share can be attained. This latter decision would no doubt please market leaders who would be happy to witness the departure of competitors, but the situation would leave smaller companies with a somewhat impossible planning dilemma.

A small company which finds that the model classifies their operation as a 'dog' should remember that the model is based on market share. More important than sales relative to competition is the profit generated on assets employed. Hence, the small company could seek paths to improve ROI by either increasing profits and/or decreasing the level of investment. One method of improving profitability is to specialize in a market sector where there are few competitors, the customer is price insensitive and high prices can be charged. This scenario is most likely to occur in a sector where customers place emphasis on quality as a key element in the purchase decision (e.g., a machine tool manufacturer who specializes in supplying advanced CNC systems to OEMs in high-technology industries). Profits may also be enhanced through the strategies of reducing operating expense or lowering the cost of goods by improvements in productivity. Decreasing the company investment might be achieved by a more effective management of working capital (e.g., having less finished goods and raw materials on hand by persuading customers to accept a longer order/delivery date cycle; reducing the level of accounts receivable by speeding up payments by debtors while concurrently lengthening the period for settlement of creditor accounts). An attempt to reduce the scale of investment in fixed assets will probably be more difficult. Nevertheless, consideration could be given to increasing the productivity of assets employed by moving to double production shifts, disposing of underutilized assets and subcontracting production to another company.

The 'problem children' in the model are so named because they are failing to make an impact equal to that of the 'rising stars' in the market. Owners of 'problem children' should consider avoiding head-to-head confrontation with their competitors' more successful products and examine alternative product strategies. If product performance is poorer, then perhaps 'de-engineering' could be used to reposition the product as being more suitable in the low price/minimal performance sector (e.g., a company that positions itself in the 'low price' sector of the personal computer market by supplying relatively out-of-date technology at low cost). If the company has the R&D skills to produce superior performance products, then an alternative strategy could be to 'up-engineer' the product and concentrate on the customers seeking a specialist performance specification (e.g., the Cray computer company who build machines for the US intelligence community and the defence industry).

Even large companies should avoid carte blanche application of the model and discontinue any products which do not fall into the 'cash cow' or 'rising star' categories. Some 'dogs' are able to survive with little promotional support and can be produced from obsolete plant and equipment that has a minimal book value. Such products (often known as 'cash dogs') are capable of revenue generation for some years and it would be financial irresponsibility to eliminate this source of profit just because of a low market share. A 'problem child' product can also be of benefit if, by its retention, the company continues to acquire additional expertise in a new area of technology (e.g., NCR's involvement in mainframe computers to acquire the expertise to support their planned move from mechanical to electronic cash tills). It would also appear that the Japanese drug industry has operated on this principle over the last twenty years. Having acquired the experience of competing against the European or American companies with 'me too' formulations, they will probably use this knowledge to ensure the successful launch of new drugs now under development, which exploit the benefits of biotechnology and genetic engineering.

CORPORATE CAPABILITY STRATEGIES

Leadership and market segmentation strategies were evolved by marketeers during the fifties and sixties when market conditions were very stable. By the mid-seventies, rising per capita expenditure and new technologies were both causing a reduction in the length of PLCs. Also, smaller companies began to recognize that a very effective way of challenging well-entrenched, larger competitors was through the introduction of new products. Under these conditions, the BCG product portfolio matrix was recognized as a powerful conceptual planning tool for finding the optimal balance of resources between products according to their position on the PLC curve.

All of the above approaches, however, are based on the somewhat simplistic assumption that most markets will continue to increase in size and that any company that decides to enter a new market sector aggressively will be successful. In fact, today's companies face increasingly complex business environments owing to such factors as political or financial instability, growth constrained by stagnating demand, shortages of raw materials, emergence of new sources of competition from overseas, and the risk of almost instant product obsolescence caused by the arrival of a new technology. Hence, it is no longer safe to forecast future market potential by merely extrapolating historic trends. Marketeers now need to evaluate issues such as:

- the stability of company share, sales patterns, prices and profitability;
- the relationship between market demand and industry production capacity;
- the rate of new product introductions and the average length of PLCs;
- the lead time and scale of investment to develop and launch major new product concepts;
- the likely behaviour of existing and potential competitors;
- the future cost of promotion to sustain current market position;
- the level of customer education and product after-care service required to support existing and new products;
- the influence of government regulations on own and competitors' operations;
- the potential impact of global economic trends on future sales;
- the costs of retaining or developing technological capability;
- the potential of emergent technology to render industry or company products obsolete.

On the basis of this type of analysis it is then possible to classify a market sector in terms of relative attractiveness to the company as an area in which to operate in the future. This analysis should be accompanied by an assessment of the internal capabilities of the organization as discussed in Chapter 3. By applying a simple factor analysis, comparing each issue against an optimal scenario and scoring performance on a scale of 1 to 10, it is possible to develop a relationship between market attractiveness and corporate capability.

In Fig. 4.5 it has been assumed that the issues concerning internal capability have been classified under the five headings of marketing, technology, finance, manufacturing and managerial systems. A perfect score would be one approaching or equal to 10. Using a simple classification of a score of 0–3 for poor, 4–6 for average and 7–10 for good, internal capability can be profiled relative to market attractiveness. In cells 1, 5 and 9, capability and market attractiveness are in balance. Cells 2, 3 and 6 indicate that the company has inadequate capability relative to market attractiveness. The reverse of this situation occurs in cells 4, 7 and 8 where the company has capability greater than that demanded by market conditions.

Profiles of the type illustrated in Fig. 4.5 can be used to create a directional marketing strategy matrix in which the relationship between capability and market attractiveness provides the basis for defining alternative marketing strategies. The fundamental concepts that form the basis for the approach were pioneered by GE Corporation of America (working in

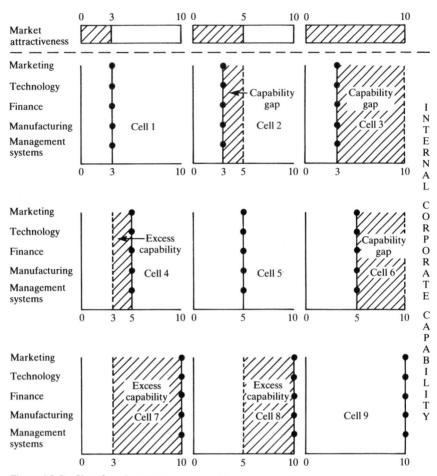

Figure 4.5 Profiles of market attractiveness and internal capability.

conjunction with the management consultancy firm of McKinsey) and by the Shell oil company in Europe. These projects were initiated because these companies needed to develop planning tools to prioritize future strategies, not just on the basis of market share as proposed in a product portfolio model but also by identifying the influence of internal strengths or weaknesses across their complete range of business activities.[11]

Use of the directional strategy approach to determine future marketing effect is illustrated in Fig. 4.6. Products which fall into cells 1, 2 and 4 offer no long-term benefits to the company, and withdrawal from the market sector will release resources for application in other areas of the company's operation. The cell 5 strategy also releases resources, but as the company is enjoying a dominant position in the market, this action will increase profits that can be used to fund products in other market sectors. The long-term

MARKET ATTRACTIVENESS

	Low	Average	High	
Low	(1) Discontinue products immediately	(2) Phased product discontinuation	(3) Major new product launch or quit	C O R P O R A T E
Average	(4) Phased product discontinuation	(5) Sustain market position	(6) Capability improvement strategy	C A P A B
High	(7) Resource disinvestment strategy	(8) Market or product diversification strategy	(9) Leadership retention strategy ('Stay ahead programmes')	I L I T Y

Figure 4.6 Directional marketing strategy matrix.

outlook for the cell 5 area of activity does mean, however, that there would be little financial advantage in attempting to expand market share.

A product in cell 3 is failing to perform in a market sector that could make a significant contribution to future revenue. However, to succeed will involve an attempt to launch a major new product if the company is to have a significant impact on potential customers. If the new approach fails, then the strategic decision should avoid any further losses by admitting defeat and quitting the market sector. Cell 7 is also a vital market sector, but the company has developed only a reasonable capability. Nevertheless, further internal improvement is possible through incremental investment on pro- grammes such as product improvements or developing more effective promotional campaigns. If necessary there is also the possibility of using outside expertise by acquisition, or joint ventures involving other organi- zations, to create new opportunities for corporate synergy.

The situation in cell 8 is that the company has capability in excess of that needed to operate in a market sector. To exploit this internal capability, product or market diversification strategies should be implemented. Ulti- mately, of course, all companies would hope to operate in a position described for cell 9, where they are in a leadership position in a highly attractive market. Having reached this position, the company must retain their lead over competition by sustained investment in new products and promotional campaigns.

It should be recognized that the above example assumed an equal level of capability across all departments within the organization. Where the analysis reveals relative weaknesses in areas outside the marketing operation, these should receive priority for actions to improve performance. Obviously the marketing group have to show a certain degree of tact in raising this issue with other department heads. One possible approach to avoid an adverse reaction is for the marketing department to offer to reduce near-term spending and thereby release funds to support investment in the capability improvement process in other areas of the company operation.

The long-term aim of all companies is for the marketing operation to be active only in market sector/capability status situations of the types specified by cells 5, 6, 8 and 9. It should be accepted however that, initially, the analysis may reveal cell 1, 2, 4 or 7 scenarios. This should not be viewed as a completely hopeless situation as long as the resources released from improved management of these poorer sectors is reinvested in market opportunities that offer greater potential over the longer term.

AN ILLUSTRATION OF THE DIRECTIONAL STRATEGY APPROACH

Brymor Ltd manufactured the components used by other companies in the UK who fabricated and installed new and replacement windows. The industry originally used aluminium as the standard material for window frames, with the first improvement being the introduction of frames containing thermal barriers which improved the heat conservation properties of double-glazed windows. Approximately half of the industry unit volume came from sales in the UK domestic household market, with the balance of demand mainly coming from industrial customers requiring products such as new shop fronts and windows for office buildings or factories.

An important trend in the domestic market over recent years had been the increasing importance of low-cost all-plastic or uPVC frames, and in the premium quality sector, the introduction of 'composite' frames made from aluminium coated with polyvinyl compounds. The industrial market, however, still considered that aluminium and thermal break frames were the most suitable products to meet their specification for durability and variability of shape.

Brymor Ltd supplied (*a*) bar lengths of all four product types (i.e., aluminium, thermal break aluminium, composite and uPVC) for use by customers who wished to fabricate windows to meet specific contracts, and (*b*) window frame kits for those customers who only wished to install frames without any involvement in fabrication. Although limited industry information prevented accurate measurement of market share, Brymor was considered as a market leader in the supply of premium quality, advanced design bar lengths and kit form products.

MARKET ATTRACTIVENESS

		Low	Average	High
	Low	(1) DISCONTINUATION No relevant product	(2) PHASED DISCONTINUATION No relevant product	(3) LAUNCH OR QUIT No relevant product
B R Y M O R C A P A B I L I T Y	Average	(4) PHASED DISCONTINUATION Aluminium products supplied to small customers in both the domestic and industrial market sectors	(5) SUSTAIN POSITION Thermal break products in the domestic market	(6) CAPABILITY IMPROVEMENT Investment in more effective manufacturing and marketing capability to attract new major uPVC customers
	High	(7) RESOURCE DISINVESTMENT Aluminium products supplied to medium/ large customers in the domestic market	(8) DIVERSIFICATION Entry in industrial market for thermal break products	(9) LEADERSHIP RETENTION Investment in new product development for composite products

Figure 4.7 Application of directional marketing strategy matrix to example company, Brymor Ltd.

Historically the company had made little attempt to determine future market opportunity. New products were produced only when time was available in the manufacturing operation. Promotional efforts were divided equally across all products, with the salesforce making calls wherever they felt an order could be obtained. In the face of increasing competition from other UK manufacturers, Brymor decided it could be beneficial to take a focused approach to marketing planning in relation to products, market opportunities and customer profitability. The first step in this new orientation was to analyse financial performance by customer. This analysis revealed that the total costs of supplying small customers, especially if they used Brymor as a secondary supplier, was almost equal to the revenue generated by this customer group.

The issues of market demand, the position of each product on the PLC, profitability by customer group and internal capability were utilized to construct a directional marketing strategy matrix (Fig. 4.7). This exercise indicated that, in future, resources should be directed towards enhancing internal capability in the uPVC domestic window sector, diversification from the domestic into the industrial market for thermal break products, and investment in development of new products to sustain the company's leadership in the composite products market sector.

REFERENCES

1. S. Schoeffler, D. Buzzell and D. F. Heany, 'Impact of strategic planning on profit performance', *Harvard Business Review*, March 1974.
2. R. D. Buzzeli, B. T. Gale and R. G. M. Sultan, 'Market share—a key to profitability', *Harvard Business Review*, January 1975.
3. J. D. C. Roach, 'From strategic planning to strategic performance: closing the achievement gap', *Outlook*, Booz Allen & Hamilton, New York, Spring 1981.
4. R. Frank, W. Massy and Y. Wind, *Market Segmentation*, Prentice-Hall, 1972.
5. R. Bonoma, I. Benson and P. Shapiro, *Segmenting Industrial Markets*, Lexington Books, 1983.
6. N. K. Dhalla and S. Yuspeh, 'Forget the product life cycle!', *Harvard Business Review*, January 1976.
7. R. Polli and V. Cook, 'Validity of the product life cycle', *Journal of Business*, October 1969.
8. R. D. Buzzell, 'Competitive behavior and product life cycles', in *New Ideas for Successful Marketing*, J. S. Wright and J. L. Goldstucker (eds), American Marketing Association, 1966.
9. B. Hedley, 'Strategy and the business portfolio', *Long Range Planning*, vol. 10, February 1977.
10. G. S. Day, 'Diagnosing the product portfolio', *Journal of Marketing*, April 1977.
11. S. J. Q. Robinson, R. E. Hitchens and D. P. Wade, 'The directional policy matrix—tool for strategic planning', *Long Range Planning*, vol. 11, June 1978.

FIVE

MANAGING NEW PRODUCTS

WHAT IS A 'NEW' PRODUCT?

Attempting to define a 'new' product is complicated by the semantic issue of 'what is "newness"?'. A manufacturer of industrial adhesives may consider a minor reformulation, which reduces setting time by 5 per cent, to be a new product. Another company in the same industry might treat this type of change as simply an improvement and only apply the word 'new' to a radically different formulation capable of bonding a much broader range of materials.

One possible solution to this discrepancy is to consider that any innovation, no matter how large or small, which is perceived by the customer as providing enhanced value, can be classified as a new product. This definition then permits all forms of innovation — from a minor packaging change through to the application of a radical technological advance — to be encompassed in an examination of the new product development process.

A MANAGEMENT MODEL FOR NEW PRODUCT DEVELOPMENT

Not all products are an immediate success, and the sales performance of others may lead to their discontinuation very early in the PLC. There are numerous factors that can influence the success or failure of any single product,[1] but whatever the reason it is important to understand that any failure represents a loss to the company of all the resources invested during the product development phase.

Most companies now accept the strategic implications of the PLC

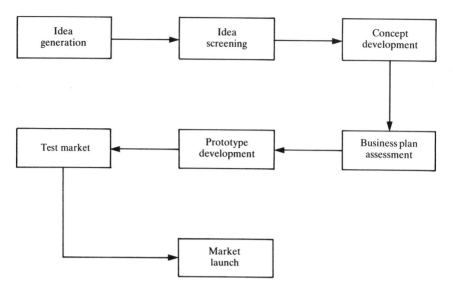

Figure 5.1 The typical control process for managing new product development.

concept and the need to remain ahead of competition by constantly seeking to enhance their portfolio of products. There is also widespread acceptance of the fact that new product development is a difficult task and the risk of failure will probably always remain very high.[2] In consequence, many organizations have established some form of structured product development process of the type illustrated in Fig. 5.1 with the objective of ensuring that only successful new products are introduced into the marketplace.[3]

The starting point is to generate numerous ideas using sources such as customers, intermediaries, suppliers, employees and the application of new technologies. During the screening phase, the management team will seek to progress only those ideas that have the capability of fulfilling predetermined corporate strategies and objectives. At the concept development stage, market research is used to determine the level of market appeal for the new product idea. Assuming this research provides evidence of potential market demand, a business plan can be prepared, defining financial performance in terms of absolute profit and ROI. If this analysis reveals an acceptable performance forecast, work will commence on the development of a product prototype. The prototype should fulfil (*a*) the expectations described by potential customers during concept evaluation and (*b*) the production costs forecasted in the business plan. The prototype will then undergo market evaluation using such techniques as customer placement studies and distribution shipment tests.

In industrial markets, the simplicity of the marketing mix to be used in the launch phase will usually mean that market introduction can commence without further research. For many consumer goods products, where the marketing mix may be more complex and the level of promotional expenditure very high (e.g., the 1989 announcement of an £8m launch budget for the new Surf liquid detergent), it may be decided to implement a test market. The purpose of this test is to assess the overall effectiveness of the proposed marketing plan in a geographically restricted area, such as a single town or television region, to obtain final validation of forecasted trial and repeat purchase rates. Should the product fail to perform at an acceptable level in the test market, the company will have avoided the much larger scale of expenditure associated with a product launch on a national scale.

MARKETEERS AND INNOVATION

Given marketeers' understanding of market trends, knowledge of market research tools and an ability to utilize the marketing mix to influence demand, it would seem quite logical for marketing departments to be assigned the responsibility for managing new products. However, if one lists the products that are considered desirable in the households of western nations — televisions, refrigerators, cars, video recorders, home computers, microwave ovens and washing machines — it is interesting to note that marketeers had little influence on the creation and introduction of the early models of most of these items. They usually became involved only after each product category had been initially introduced to the world, when companies wished to increase their share of sales in a particular market sector.

New product development is about innovation. It should be of concern, therefore, to realize that, as demonstrated by the Booz Allen study (Table 5.1), marketeers' involvement in new products will mean that the majority of financial and time resources are committed to marginal product changes or improvements. In consequence, virtually no marketing department effort is expended on major scale innovation through which a company is able to dramatically improve its market share over the longer term.

Some of the larger multinationals have already recognized that their marketing operation is not always very competent when it comes to effectively managing innovation. To overcome this weakness they may rely increasingly upon alternative processes such as (a) acquisition of smaller, more innovative companies, (b) purchasing the rights to patents or licences and (c) hiring the services of new product consultants to rejuvenate their marketing programmes.

Some corporations, having identified a poor track record within their marketing operation, have created completely new autonomous systems through which to stimulate a greater level of innovation.[4] In America, for example, Kodak have established an 'office of innovation network' (OIN) designed to stimulate all staff within the organization to come forward with

Table 5.1 Allocation of activity across various aspects of the new product management process

Proportion of corporate effort*	Type of activity	Level of innovation
11%	Cost reduction—existing products	Low
7%	Repositioning—existing products	Low
26%	Improved performance—existing products	Low
26%	Line extension—existing products	Low
Total: 70%	Low-level innovation programmes	Low
20%	Products new to the company	Medium
10%	Products new to the world	High

*Source of data: New Products for the 1980s, Booz, Allen & Hamilton, 1982.

new ideas. A similar concept has been introduced by the Xerox Corporation, which they have labelled an 'innovation opportunity programme' (IOP). The IOP has been assigned the role of assisting originators of ideas to further develop their concepts. This is achieved by making available advice, managerial support and resources in an environment removed from the day-to-day affairs that might stifle innovative thinking. It is necessary to recognize, however, that Kodak and Xerox have created these 'innovation centres' with the specific aim of stimulating change across all aspects of their organizational activities. The centres, therefore, have a responsibility greater than merely to stimulate new product development.

If companies begin to manage their innovation activities through autonomous centres, marketeers must recognize that resources previously allocated to their department may be diverted away to support these new initiatives. If marketeers wish to halt this erosion of their responsibility, the underlying factors causing them to fail as their prime source of major product innovation within the organization must be understood and then remedied.

ORGANIZATIONAL BARRIERS TO INNOVATION

Career-minded executives will constantly strive to be assigned to projects or roles that are seen to be important to their superiors within the organization. Role importance can often be measured by 'indirect indicators' such as position of a work group in the organizational hierarchy, salary levels of group leaders, office size, priority in the allocation of scarce corporate resources and even 'being granted a key to the executive toilet'.

In some companies, one finds that new products do not even warrant creation of a separate operating identity. Instead, the role is assigned to the existing products marketing group as a secondary responsibility to be carried out on a 'when time permits' basis.[5] Even where the company has created a new product group, it is frequently the case that the group's authority over service resources (e.g., access to the market research department; time with the advertising agency) is rarely equal to that held by the marketing managers responsible for existing products. These latter individuals can often retain control by (*a*) claiming their activities will have a more immediate impact on revenue/profit generation and (*b*) using their much larger operating budgets to gain the loyalty of suppliers such as the advertising agency and packaging design consultants.[6]

In those organizations in which the new products group has been given adequate authority over resources, one will possibly find that the paths to promotion within the company indicate that the marketeer should not become too closely associated with new products for any significant period of time.[7] An example of this situation is to be found in many of the 'blue chip' fast moving consumer goods (FMCG) companies where the typical career path is progression from graduate trainee to assistant brand manager on an established brand, then brand manager for new products and finally brand manager for an existing major product with a significant promotional budget. In these circumstances, a corporate culture may be created where new product managers are pleased when technical problems necessitate a postponement of the product launch. This event may cause senior management to advance the decision to promote the young manager to his first established brand in order to ensure that the individual remains engaged in a productive role.

IDEA GENERATION AND ORGANIZATIONAL STRUCTURE

Successful innovation depends upon maximizing the breadth of sources capable of generating product ideas which are genuinely new to the world and not merely an attempt to improve on an established product that has been around for many years. Unfortunately the prime objective of a system of the type shown in Fig 5.1 is to minimize the possibility that a potential failure is progressed through to the launch phase. In consequence, this form of 'avoidance of failure' control system may result in insufficient emphasis being given to the idea generation process and does little to promote the need for really innovative thinking within the organization.

As demonstrated in Fig. 5.2, a huge variety of sources can be used to stimulate the process of generating ideas for the new product. To exploit all these sources, it is important to understand that new product development is actually composed of numerous subdevelopment pathways, ranging from the updating of existing products to sustain a competitive advantage in mature markets through to operating at the frontier of a new technology where, initially, no immediate marketing opportunity is apparent to the researcher.

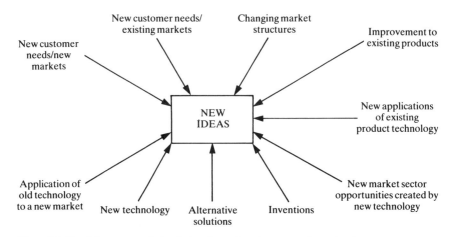

Figure 5.2 Possible sources of stimulation for actions in new product planning.

In order to handle this complexity of pathways, it is necessary to create a new product organization structure of the type shown in Fig. 5.3.[8]

The objective of the structure proposed in Fig. 5.3 is to focus all efforts on a coordinated approach to the exploitation of all aspects of both market and product opportunities. One of the most controversial aspects of the structure is the inclusion of an acquisitions group within the new product operation. Traditionally, acquisitions have either been the domain of the corporate planning department or have existed as a separate entity reporting directly to the Board. The risk of using structures such as these is that acquisition may be considered on a solely financial basis, namely whether the action will enhance corporate profitability. Unfortunately this philosophy can result in acquisitions being made which are not compatible with existing marketing strategies. Excessive senior management time may then have to be directed towards integrating the newly purchased business into the overall corporate operations.

Another unusual aspect of Fig. 5.3 is the inclusion of a 'new technology group'. This proposal is designed to overcome the problem encountered in most organizations where the marketing group are asked to contribute to R&D programmes at a very late stage in the product commercialization process.[9] The approach is known as 'downstream coupling'. The risk is that the company research division may have only limited access to market intelligence about customer needs. In these circumstances, opportunities may be missed to match customer requirements with actual performance of products still under development.

For the organizational structure in Fig. 5.3 to be successful, the attitudes of some marketeers must change. First, they have to accept that they may lack certain skills, especially in areas such as understanding technology or

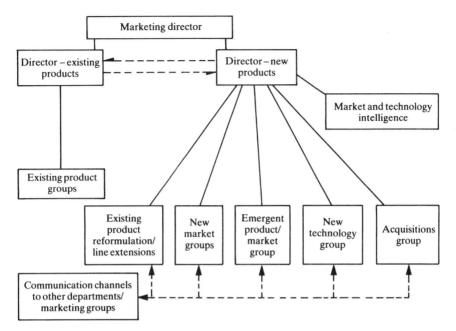

Figure 5.3 Possible organizational structure to provide multifaceted product development.

selecting potential acquisition opportunities. This will require importing specialists from other functional areas into the marketing operation, who then require some training in various aspects of marketing management (e.g., accountants experienced in acquisitions needing to comprehend the relationship between current market/product mix and target purchases; engineers who must develop an understanding of product technology in relation to the potential operating problems faced by customers).

Another important change is for senior marketing staff to select their best middle/junior managers for appointment to the new product operation. This contrasts with the usual approach of placing the best staff in the existing product management groups. The latter philosophy is a significant waste of human resources because existing products can often be sustained by less able managers. Even more importantly, assigning the best managers to existing products undermines the credibility of the claim that new products are a priority area capable of controlling the future destiny of the organization. Ultimately the company must reach the point where (*a*) the most probable path for a successful career is through the new product operation and (*b*) new products are seen to be the main source of employees who will progress to more senior management positions over the long term.

The final change in operating philosophy is for marketeers and senior management to understand that certain aspects of the new product process will require a much longer period than the six- to twelve-month schedules

Table 5.2   Matrix analysis for book products

Markets	Functions	Technologies	Products
Children	Data storage	Printed word	Books
Adults	Communication	Microfiche	Computers
Industry	Knowledge	Electronic memory	Video recorders
Education	Leisure	Film	Magazines
	Skills aids	Tape	Microfilm
		Painting	Tape recorders
			Record players
			Telephone

allotted for simple product reformulation or repositioning projects. Unfortunately, marketing is a functional area of management which seems to attract individuals who prefer short-term problems as this permits them to be involved in a series of projects over a comparatively short time. This attitude is not compatible with longer term R&D projects where progress is dependent upon the progressive solution of complex, interacting technological problems. Hence, in selecting project leaders for new product programmes, care must be taken to choose individuals who have the ability to sustain their own motivation and that of subordinates over periods that could range from two to possibly ten years.

INNOVATIVE PROBLEM-SOLVING

In our personal and our working lives most of us have encountered a product or a solution to a problem and immediately thought 'Now why didn't I think of that?' The answer is that we probably attempted to apply an old solution to a changing situation where a new approach was demanded. Or, in other words, we have failed to act as an 'innovative problem solver'.

The human mind has the capability for logical and intuitive thinking, and both of these faculties can be used to solve problems. Logical thinking involves a sequential, step-by-step process, whereas intuition is a holistic approach in which solutions are visualized in their entirety.[10] Over the last few years, various techniques have been developed that can assist marketeers to more effectively exploit these two approaches when thinking about new products.[11]

Aids to more insightful logical thought are known as linear techniques and include methods such as matrix analysis, morphological analysis, attribute listing and design trees. Each of them is appropriate to certain situations. Matrix analysis is applied where one wishes to stimulate a deeper examination of the relationship between two variables such as markets and product benefits or product performance and technologies.[12] Table 5.2

Table 5.3 Attribute listing for houseplants

Attribute	New opportunity
Pot	Variety of containers to suit homeowners' decors
Soil	Artificial material containing balanced nutrients for plants
Leaves	Genetic manipulation to increase size or vary colours
Stem	Genetic manipulation to strengthen stem and grow taller plants
Flowers	Genetic manipulation to increase frequency of flowering during year

illustrates the process that might occur if a publishing company wished to determine possible relationships between the various benefits offered by books relative to different market sectors.

Faced with the need to create a broader understanding of a product or market, another very useful technique is attribute listing.[13] Each attribute, once identified, can be examined to see if an improvement in the attribute could lead to a new customer opportunity. An example of the approach for houseplants is given in Table 5.3.

Attribute listing can provide the basis for expanding on an idea by the construction of a decision tree. The objective of the tree is to stimulate thought about pathways through which to identify new product or market opportunities. An example of a tree to extend the artifical soil idea identified by attribute listing is given in Fig. 5.4.

Techniques to enhance intuitive thinking are designed to stimulate the mind to leapfrog over logic and generate a complete solution. Three common techniques to stimulate intuition are brainstorming, imagery and visualization. Of the three, brainstorming is probably the best known. It uses the concept of stimulating the generation of as many ideas as possible.[14] To aid the process it is often executed in a group situation, led by a facilitator. As the objective of brainstorming is to maximize creativity, it is important that contributors avoid any form of evaluation of their own or others' ideas until

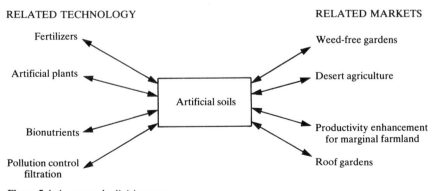

Figure 5.4 An example division tree.

the session is over. At that stage the list of ideas can be reviewed to determine whether there is new product synergy from linking together two or more of the ideas that have been mentioned. Imagery also requires that the mind is not inhibited while ideas are being generated. The technique achieves this by relying on the development of a meditative approach such as being very relaxed, using deep-breathing exercises, and gradually moving from the edge to the centre of a problem. The contributors are instructed to let the specified issues evolve into symbols or pictures in their mind. By discussing these 'mind' pictures, one can move forward to isolate new solutions or opportunities.[4]

The mind tends to function more easily using symbols or impressions rather than using words. The visualization technique exploits this fact by the individual being guided to draw a picture to describe their thoughts on a relevant theme (e.g., 'what markets will be available in the year 2000?'). To stimulate the process, the individual may be guided by an agenda, developing additions to the picture as each issue is considered. Once the drawing has been completed, the individual then reflects on possible alternative solutions that might be contained or prompted by the visualization.[4]

WORKING IN TEAMS

In an increasingly complex world, the principle that 'two minds are better than one' is often very valid in the new product development process. It is therefore imperative that once marketeers have evolved a personal creative thinking style they then bring this attribute into group-based activities. Unfortunately some marketeers exhibit a dominant, control-taking management style and this is guaranteed to block group creativity. To avoid this situation, the marketeer must aim to achieve the following objectives for a new product development team:

- frank and supportive exchange of opinions;
- minimal conflict when resolving different viewpoints;
- common objectives shared by the entire team;
- consensus decision-making and planning;
- sharing of expertise and total commitment to project, not personal, success;
- sharing of the glory from success with all individuals who have been involved in a project.

In some situations the marketeer will be head of a project, requiring leadership skills such as delegation, motivating others, dispute resolution, allocating resources and sustaining group purpose or morale. It is just as likely, however, that the marketeer will be a member of a development team. This role is just as difficult, demanding such skills as constructive criticism, assertive communication and self-responsibility.

Where an organization is moving to, or has adopted, team-based new product development structures, the issue of developing effective interpersonal managerial skills within the marketing group is vital. The company must create a system of monitoring managerial performance among the team members, and where areas of weakness are identified, must take immediate remedial action through training programmes and self-development schemes. Where these actions fail to remedy the performance problem, consideration should be given to restructuring the membership of the project team.

NEW PRODUCT SUCCESS

New products are vital to the long-term success of all organizations. The tendency of some senior management is to believe that technological problems or incorrect marketing planning decisions are the reason for product failures. Although their diagnosis may be valid in certain situations, equally probable causes are inappropriate organizational structures, executive reward systems which emphasize short-term achievements, and insufficient efforts to maximize the level of innovative problem-solving by marketeers.

Companies who have recognized the importance of the latter factors, and have taken steps to remove these obstacles, are more likely to reap the benefits from new product development programmes than organizations who are still taking a more traditional approach to this area of managerial responsibility.

REFERENCES

1. H. Lazo, 'Finding the key to success in new product failures', *Industrial Marketing*, vol. 50, November 1965.
2. M. Crawford, 'Marketing research and the new product failure rate', *Journal of Marketing*, vol. 41, No. 2, April 1977.
3. R. D. Hisrick and M. P. Peters, *Marketing Decisions for New and Mature Products*, Bell & Howell, 1984.
4. S. Majaro, *The Creative Gap*, Longman, 1988.
5. P. Stein, 'The role of the product manager in new product development', *Marketing News*, vol. 1, October 1972.
6. R. T. Hise and P. Kelly, 'Product management on trial', *Journal of Marketing*, vol. 42, No. 4, October 1978.
7. S. R. Gemmel and D. L. Wileman, 'The product manager as an influence agent', *Journal of Marketing*, vol. 35, October 1969.
8. T. Haller, 'An organisational structure to help you in the 80's', *Advertising Age*, August 1983.
9. W. B. Brown and L. N. Goslin, 'R&D conflict: manager versus scientist', *Business Topics*, vol. 75, Summer 1965.

10. Y. T. Li, D. G. Janoson and E. D. Gravalho, *Technological Innovation in Education and Industry*, Van Nostrand Reinholdt, 1980.
11. E. Debano, *Lateral Thinking for Managers: A Handbook for Creativity*, American Management Association, 1971.
12. C. H. Clark, *Idea Management: How to Motivate Creativity and Innovation*, AMACOM, 1980.
13. S. J. Parnes and H. F. Harding (eds), *A Source Book for Creative Thinking*, Scribner, 1962.
14. M. O. Edwards, 'Solving problems creatively', *Journal of Systems Management*, vol. 17, No. 1, January 1966.

SIX

MARKETING TACTICS

THE LESSON OF THE FIRST WORLD WAR

As the concept of the strategic approach to managing organizations has gained in popularity, academics and researchers have noticed areas of distinct similarity between running a successful business and the principles of military strategic planning. This has stimulated a number of individuals to propose that the theories of warfare management can be applied to enhancing the effectiveness of the marketing planning process.[1,2,3]

One of the most traumatic events that influenced modern military thinking was the First World War where, on the Western Front in Europe, both sides learned the futility of massive frontal assaults on a well-entrenched defending force. In those companies where the majority of products fall within the 'dog' classification under the BCG matrix system, the usual objective is to endeavour to steal share from the more successful companies in the market. Many of these attempts to gain sales will involve frontal assaults on the market leaders, and the result similarly reflects that of the tragic management of the Western Front during the First World War.

By mounting a frontal assault, the attacker will come in contact with the opponent's strongest areas of defence. Classic military theory proposes that a superiority in resources of attacker over defender should be in the range of 3:1. In the case of marketing battles, superiority can be achieved using various combinations of product performance, creation of a distinctive market position, pricing and the promotional spending. Prior to initiating a new campaign, however, detailed market intelligence must be gathered in order to determine how best to utilize various elements within the marketing mix. Two recent examples of how this approach can be used are provided by ICI's Dulux paints and Courage Brewery's Hofmeister lager.

By the late seventies, Dulux's leadership position in the all-important white emulsion sector of the domestic paints market had been eroded by aggressive price-promotion and emphasis on own brands by the UK multiples and DIY chains.[4] Research revealed that Dulux was mainly of appeal to older, up-market males who were no longer an important buying group in the market. The company developed a new range of tinted white paints to be introduced under the banner of 'Whiter Shade of Pale', designed to create excitement across all age groups, but with particular appeal to women. The 1982 launch included a £2.8 million television campaign, £0.4 million point of sale promotions and featured the 'Dulux Dog' as a brand identification mechanism. The new range added 18 share points to the Dulux business and, just as importantly, had minimal adverse impact on the company's traditional white emulsion sales.

Lager is the most rapidly growing segment in the UK beer industry. Hofmeister was a late entry into the market. Research in 1983 indicated low brand awareness (25 versus 57 per cent for the leader Carlsberg) and revealed a poor score for key attributes such as flavour, quality and taste[4] versus competition. Young people are the heaviest user group for lagers and it was concluded that there was a need to reposition the brand as being perceived as 'cool and fashionable' by the 18–25 age group. This was achieved by a very effective promotional campaign which featured 'George the Bear' as a stylish, sophisticated, Fonz-type, street-smart animal as the leader of his young peer group (i.e., the same self-image desired by young lager drinkers). During the first year of the new campaign, overall lager sales rose by 9 per cent whereas Hofmeister enjoyed a massive 25 per cent increase in sales.

The number of successful frontal assaults based on minor reformulation or product positioning changes is unfortunately much lower than cases where companies failed in their attempt to capture share from a more powerful competitor. Detailed information on the cause of failure is not easy to find. Hence one has to rely on clues such as press releases indicating that 'Mr X the marketing director has recently tendered his resignation' or 'Company Y has decided to undertake a rationalization of certain areas of its operations'. Where further information is available, it is frequently found to be the case that the company attempted to mount a frontal assault with an inferior product concept and/or insufficient promotional spending compared to other brands in the market.

Recent examples of this type of failure are illustrated by:

- Eddie Shah's attempt to launch his new national newspaper *Today*;
- Rowntree Mackintosh's departure from the snack food market in 1988, only six years after their acquisition of Sooner Foods;
- the prestigious London toy store Hamleys in 1987/88 who were unsuccessful in their attempt to open a chain of regional stores in other areas of the UK.

Given the frequent announcement of staff departures and product rationalization in the trade press, there is a need to explain why marketeers continue to become involved in frontal assaults. One possible reason is that they value—like those First World War generals—the excitement of being in control of others and the 'glory' that will accrue if the assault is successful. Another possible reason is that some marketeers have yet to appreciate that there are other marketing tactics available that can be used in the place of a 'head-to-head' confrontation with a more powerful enemy. Battle tactics which may prove more effective than an approach equivalent to the classic 'Charge of the Light Brigade' attempted by the British army at Balaclava in 1854 include flanking, envelopment, isolation and guerilla warfare (explained in a later section). These tactics can be applied in isolation or combined during the campaign to defeat the competition. A key advantage of these alternative approaches is that because the attack is directed at less well-defended areas of the competitor's operation, the level of resources needed to mount the offensive is usually lower than that required for a frontal assault. Hence, if the attack is successful, the company will have resources sufficient to exploit further growth opportunities or stave off any counter-offensive. Alternatively, should the attack fail, the company will not be weakened to the point of becoming easy prey to a competitive response.

NON-CONFRONTATIONAL ATTACK

A competitor's defences will be strongest in the market sector where an attack is most expected. Thus the 'thinking' marketeer should seek out an area or 'flank' where the enemy is weakest. Both the Germans and the Japanese car manufacturers used this approach in America. Instead of attempting to compete directly with large, family cars produced by Ford and General Motors, they concentrated on the smaller, fuel-efficient car sector. To a certain extent it must be recognized that the attackers were aided by the unusual ally of OPEC in the mid-seventies, who very kindly strengthened the validity of the small car proposition in America by creating the oil crisis that drove up petrol prices.

An example of a service industry flank attack is that of the Trustee Savings Bank (TSB) in the mid-eighties when they realized that the major UK High Street banks mainly relied upon recommendations from parents and promotions directed at college students to attract new account holders. The TSB developed a marketing campaign directed specifically at 15–19 year olds who were leaving school and going directly into employment. The theme of the TSB advertising was 'the bank which likes to say yes'. Further under-pinning of their flank positioning was achieved through mechanisms such as a free magazine mailed to teenagers and a discount card valid on purchases through Virgin Records. Launched in 1984, within two years the flank attack trebled the bank's share of the 16–20 year olds opening their first bank account.[5]

Some flank attacks will require the company to invest in new product technology prior to battle commencing. Following the 1980 UK Government decision to allow competition with British Telecom, Mercury Communications entered the market. It appeared on the surface to be a somewhat uneven battle: British Telecom having over £10 billion in assets and enjoying a virtual monopoly position in the UK telecommunications market.

Mercury selected those sectors of the business market where speed, efficiency and quality of service were significantly more important than price (e.g., financial institutions in the City of London, brokerage houses and multinational corporations). Backed by their parent company, Cable and Wireless, Mercury invested heavily in advanced communications technology to provide the basis of their superiority of service claim over competition. Establishment of a beach-head in the early years was not easy, but by 1990 the company is forecasted to achieve annual sales of at least £500 million.[6]

The flank segment approach is based upon identifying an opportunity in an existing market that is not well defended. The same philosophy can be used to find an area of a country or part of the world where the competition is not strongly entrenched. This is known as a geographical flank attack. The UK engineering conglomerate GEC have used this approach against other European and American heavy turbine manufacturers by identifying the future opportunities in the equipping of new power stations in the mainland China market and entering this area of the world ahead of competition.

Flank attacks focus on an edge of a competitor's business and aim to establish a strong beach-head before an adequate counter-attack can be organized. Unless the flanking move is very powerful, the defender will still remain a successful supplier in prime market sectors. If the attacker wishes to alter this situation, then this may be possible through an encirclement move where the attacker launches simultaneous offensives on a number of fronts. A classic example of a successful application of this concept has been the Seiko watch company. This organization created a portfolio of watches to cover all price/quality combinations and then overwhelmed competitors on a global basis by building distribution in all sectors of retailing from discount houses through to up-market jewellers.

Encirclement requires a major investment in product development and promotional programmes. Hence the tactic is rarely utilized because of the massive financial risk to the attacker if the offensive is repulsed. Where a company has only limited resources, encirclement may still be possible if the defender has adopted a complacent attitude and ignores a slowly developing encirclement attack. Vlasic Pickle was an American regional pickle producer which managed to execute this approach against the giant Heinz Corporation. The management at Vlasic recognized that strong regional taste preferences existed among consumers. The company embarked on an acquisition programme to buy companies, similar to themselves, which also had a market strength in a limited geographic area. Initially these new companies were left to operate independently of each other until Vlasic had built market coverage across most of the US. They then used this distribution and resource base to launch a national promotional campaign linked to localized, low-cost sales promotion activity. The move came as a surprise to Heinz who faced massive share losses to the Vlasic Corporation.[7]

Where the competitor is strongly entrenched and will react violently to an attack at any point along its marketing front, the attacker is likely to be overwhelmed by the ferocity of the counter-attack. In these circumstances, the attacker may wish to consider a leapfrog strategy to bypass a competitor's defence systems. The Avon company used this approach to great effect upon recognizing the potential risks of competing at store level with other cosmetic companies in America. Instead of confronting these organizations by distributing Avon goods through the traditional retail outlets, the company created the famous 'Avon calling' salesforce which took the brand into the homes of the customers.

In many cases leapfrogging is only made possible by the application of new technology which causes the competitive product to appear to be obsolete. At the beginning of 1984, the UK retail colour television market was dominated by Thorn EMI and Philips. Despite heavy promotional spending, Toshiba was only able to achieve a share of 3 per cent. Market research indicated that the brand suffered from low awareness and an unfavourable image. The company recognized that a head-to-head confront-ation would not be successful and therefore decided to leapfrog the com-petition by introducing their new flat square tube (FST) technology into the UK market. FST was recognized as the most significant development in television technology since the introduction of colour. Using an advertising campaign which communicated the benefit that FST gave a better picture than conventional televisions, by the end of 1985 Toshiba had become the fourth largest brand in the UK colour television market.[5]

Another option for an attacker is to mount small intermittent attacks on the competitors with the aim of weakening them to the point where it is possible to establish a permanent foothold in the market. Guerilla warfare of this type is most attractive to small companies who lack the resources to mount a large-scale assault on the market. Conventional military wisdom suggests that if the attacker wishes to gain a permanent market territory, the company must eventually be prepared to move to more conventional methods in order to achieve its objective. Nevertheless, the tactic is extremely popular with small regional organizations who lack resources to ever move to the second phase of the offensive. Their future is dependent upon remaining of such minor significance that the larger national company competition cannot be bothered to retaliate.

Guerilla warfare is often used in the computer software industry, where a small specialist firm concentrates on the provision of customer-tailored management systems for clients who are not satisfied with the performance of software available from the national suppliers. Occasionally, however, 'from such small acorns, oak trees can grow'. This effect has been demonstrated by the Reuters company who have applied their understanding of handling news on a global scale to now providing specialist information services for the rapidly burgeoning financial services industry.

Military history is littered with examples of attacking armies whose speed of advance outstripped their support services (e.g., the German invasion of Russia in the Second World War). Extended lines of communication then offer ripe targets for flanking counter-attacks. Military theorists, therefore, stress the need to assess accurately what constitutes a manageable territorial target before the attack commences. The same situation should concern the marketeer. In developing a plan, the company must determine the level of market share it can sustain, which in many cases will be influenced by those internal resources that are in short supply. For example, during the 1988/89 UK economic recovery, a number of consulting firms found that clients were contacting them for specialist services (e.g., installing JIT production systems; introducing total quality programmes) but they had insufficient consulting staff qualified to implement all the assignments being offered.

HOLDING ON TO WHAT YOU HAVE

Preparing and implementing a plan to attract customers from a competitor or enter a new market sector is a very appealing activity for the marketeer. What probably seems more mundane (but nevertheless equally important) is holding onto the company's existing sales base. To fulfil this objective, it is necessary for marketeers to pay as much attention to developing effective defence tactics as they do to planning campaigns for growth.

In designing defence systems, three objectives should be borne in mind:

- Do not lose any sales to competition.
- Inflict such severe damage on an attacker that their future market position is undermined.
- Where possible, seek an opportunity to make a counter-attack that will generate incremental profit at minimal risk or diversion of internal resources.

The commonest form of defence is to establish an area of territory in the market and to surround this position with one or more protective barriers. A very powerful defence barrier is the ability to deliver the greatest level of product or service quality at the lowest possible cost. This provides the company with the option of (*a*) having a high price and using the profit/unit of sale to fund heavy promotional activity or (*b*) being able to react to competition by using aggressive pricing policies. This 'cost leadership' form of defence is usually restricted to large organizations who have developed economies of scale in purchasing, manufacturing, marketing or distribution (e.g., the multinational oil companies; national supermarket chains).

Military strategists are very aware of the hazards of assuming that a well-defended position is impregnable as this attitude can lull the defender into a false sense of security (e.g., the infamous Maginot Line built by the French which proved useless in the face of the 1940 *blitzkrieg* tactics of the German Panzer groups). The same risk faces companies who establish a cost leadership position and then fail to reinvest in an ongoing programme of upgrading corporate productivity or product innovation.

After a while the organization will become incapable of responding effectively to a well-planned campaign from an aggressor. Post-war examples are to be found in the European camera and electronics industries. Both of these groups found their dominant market position eroded by innovative competitors from the Far East, and in many cases when they realized the need to respond, they lacked the product technology to mount an effective counter-offensive.

For companies who do not have the resources to create a position of defence based on cost leadership, another approach can be to establish a perceived uniqueness about the product that competitors find extremely difficult to duplicate. The uniqueness of Rolls Royce cars, for example, is that of limited production, maintenance of a quality image and the marketing of the product through a very select group of distributors. This has created an 'exclusivity' positioning which protects them from competition in virtually every market in the world. Another defence tactic is to exploit the positive image of being the originator of a product that establishes a market standard for quality and value. Levi Strauss, after some unsuccessful attempts to diversify into new areas of the fashion industry, has recently returned to the product originator position to effectively defend their sales in the highly competitive denim jeans market.[8]

When designing business defence strategies, the marketeer would do well to remember the military adage that 'the best form of defence is attack'. One possible approach is that of 'mobile defence' where the company is continually protecting its market position by introducing product improvements or replacement products just when the competition think they are beginning to succeed. A classic exponent of this tactic is Gillette who launch new shaving systems just as other companies introduce duplications of existing Gillette technology: in the sixties, Gillette introduced Techmatic, followed in the early seventies by Trac II, and the Atra system at the end of the decade.[9] Another well-known practitioner of the mobile defence philosophy is the IBM Corporation. They have for many years successfully updated their computer systems at the time when the competition were beginning to make inroads into the market by offering lower cost IBM clones.

A well-planned continuous updating of product portfolios will require a significant reinvestment of corporate profits into research, development and market testing. It will also mean that newer products will sometimes cannibalize sales of existing products and possibly hasten the speed of the latter's demise on the PLC curve. Some managers may decide that, in the face of pressure from shareholders and financial institutions for high near-term profits, the marketing department should only commit efforts to supporting existing products. Unfortunately, marketeers in both the USA and Europe who seek to avoid confrontation that could impair their own prospects for advancement, have frequently acceded to such pressures from the Board room. Although profits will remain high for a few years under this type of regime, the company's market position eventually begins to weaken as product superiority is eroded by more innovative competitors. Once this has occurred, the massive cost of re-establishing market position based upon launching new products offering performance superiority will often be well beyond the financial capability of the organization. An example of this is British Leyland (now Austin Rover) which for years continued to market the same range of cars, in general making only minor style changes every year in order to sustain buyer interest in new models. The same strategy was being used by Vauxhall, and both companies lost share in their home market. In 1981, however, Vauxhall launched the General Motors Cavalier 'world car', followed by the smaller Astra/Nova range and the executive Carlton model. By the mid-eighties Vauxhall moved to number 2 in the UK car market and British Leyland slipped to third place for the first time in the company's history. Only through massive reinvestment, product development and organizational restructuring of the type now being implemented, can British Leyland ever expect to regain market share.

The majority of defensive programmes result from the marketing group identifying a new competitive threat and then mounting an appropriate counter-offensive. The simplest forms of counter-response are revisions in sales promotions programmes or pricing policy. A change in pricing is possibly the easiest and most rapid form of response to any attack. The risk, however, is that the company may trigger off a price war. Typically the only real beneficiary of this event is the customer, who is able to purchase the product at or below cost until the warring companies call a truce or one of the combatants is forced out of the market. Pricing, therefore, must be judged as a rather crude form of defence and one that should be avoided in most circumstances.

There is a similar risk facing a company that uses sales promotions involving discounts, 'price pack' or high value redeemable coupons in response to an attack. This action can lead to a spiralling in the value of the offers made by the various combatants and may ultimately severely erode the profitability of these organizations (e.g., the 'Bingo wars' between the UK tabloid newspapers in the mid-eighties during their battle to steal circulation from each other). Even more importantly, as with price wars, the customer may be left with a lower perception of the quality/value image of the products because their attention has been directed towards price, not performance, as the basis for the purchase decision. Hence, counter-offensive tactics that sustain the quality image are to be preferred. This is more likely to occur where mechanisms such as product improvements, revision in advertising strategies or increasing the professionalism of the salesforce are used to blunt the impact of an attack.

By the early eighties, the Walls company found that their market position was under increasing threat from the growth of own-label ice cream brands in the UK retail food market. The company determined that there was an opportunity to exploit potential demand for a dessert which offered adults a more sophisticated ice cream product. To achieve this objective, the company developed a new technology which permitted layers of ice cream to be interleaved with other substances such as chocolate. The manufacturing process was sufficiently unique and complex that the company were granted patents and design registration which provided a significant defence against the technology being copied by a competitor.

The first product which exploited the technology, Viennetta, was tested in the Anglia television region. Early results indicated that the product was not cannibalising other Walls products and the company moved from a 28 to 35 per cent of the market share in less than a year. The same result was achieved during the national launch in 1983, except that not only did Viennetta improve the company market share, it actually returned the brand to a leadership position in the UK.[2]

It must be understood by the marketeer, however, that the product-based counter-offensive will involve significant investment in the product development and market launch process. Should the improvement fail in the market, the company will be left in a weaker financial position than if no attempt had been made to counter competitive pressures. The Sinclair company had an impressive track record during the early years of the UK personal computer market, offering low-cost systems in the most price-sensitive sectors of the market. However, in order to sustain market position, the company attempted to introduce new models such as the Sinclair QL range that failed to gain anywhere near the level of market acceptance that had been achieved by their earlier generation of computers. Eventually this situation forced the company into a very weakened financial position as their market share began to fall dramatically.

In consumer goods markets, a counter-offensive based on new advertising campaigns or increased media spending can usually be implemented more rapidly than the introduction of an improved product. New advertising campaigns are therefore the most popular form of counter-response to a competitor's attack if the company decides to ignore a price or sales promotion-based defence. In some cases the new advertising campaign may be based on the premise of outspending competition on a massive scale. Barclays Bank during the mid-eighties had gained significant market share in the UK consumer banking sector through the introduction of innovative products such as Saturday banking, child saver accounts and personalized bank counsellors. The eventual reaction of their main competitor, National Westminster Bank, was to increase significantly their expenditure on television advertising in order to promote their claim of being the 'Action Bank'. They would appear to have made few changes to their banking services (although some competitors felt that the bank may have altered guidelines on lending policies). It therefore seems that, through weight of advertising expenditure alone, the counter-response to Barclays was sufficient to move National Westminster to a market leadership position in the UK retail banking market.[10]

Although weight of promotional expenditure will often be the main determinant in deciding the outcome of a counter-attack, the impact of the campaign can be greatly enhanced by the ability of the advertising message to create a stronger registration of brand name and/or product benefit. In the UK lawnmower market some years ago, producers of the traditional rotary cylinder mowers such as Qualcast faced intense competition from the new technology hover products marketed by Flymo. Part of the reason for Qualcast's ability to mount a successful counter-attack was due to the encapsulation of their benefit claim in the promise 'It's a lot less bovver than a hover'. This approach effectively highlighted the hover machine's weakness of leaving grass cuttings behind on the lawn.

Marketeers seem to have a natural preference for using promotional counter-response tactics over any other approach. It is worth remembering, however, that to win on the sole basis of a new advertising campaign presents the company with two risks, one immediate and the other more long term. The immediate risk is that the competitors may respond by initiating an advertising war based on outspending the defender. Ultimately the outcome will be determined by who runs out of money first, and this is usually the smaller organization. The longer term risk is that the marketing department begins to become so confident about the power of advertising that little effort is directed behind product development or new market entry programmes. Eventually, of course, a competitor will arrive using product innovation to spearhead its attack and the defender who depends solely on advertising will be unable to block this new threat.

REFERENCES

1. A. Reis and J. Trout, *Marketing Warfare*, McGraw-Hill, 1986.
2. B. James, *Business Wargames*, Penguin, 1985.

3. P. Kotler and R. Singh, 'Marketing warfare in the 1980s', *Journal of Business Strategy*, Fall 1980.
4. C. Channon (ed.), *Advertising Works*, vol. 3, Holt Rinehart & Winston, 1985.
5. C. Channon (ed.), *Advertising Works*, vol. 4, Cassell, 1987.
6. 'Mercury turns up the heat', *Marketing Business*, vol. 4, April 1989.
7. *McKinsey Quarterly*, Spring 1981.
8. 'Jeans: the ultimate consumer durable', *Marketing Week*, February 1989.
9. *The Economist*, 10 April 1982.
10. 'Banking: strong ground for creative growth', *Marketing Week*, June 1988.

SEVEN

PRICING, PROMOTION AND DISTRIBUTION DECISIONS

MARKETING MIX AND CORPORATE STRATEGY

When confronted with a complex problem, most of us have a natural inclination to break it down into smaller, more manageable subissues. In the case of marketing problems, this can lead to overly simplistic solutions that do not take into account the potential interaction between the various elements of the marketing mix. For example, a manufacturer of competitively priced consumable office supplies, sold through local distributors in the lower end of the market, has obtained a UK licence for a technologically advanced 16-mm microfiche document storage/retrieval system. The intention is merely to support the product launch by participating in more office machine trade exhibitions. This simplistic promotional decision fails to encompass such factors as the difference in target users and the current customer base, the possible need for a different distribution system (e.g., appointment of specialist sole agency distributors) and development of new skills within the salesforce. It is therefore highly probable that the new venture will be a failure.

A fundamental objective of the marketeer is the effective management of the product portfolio to exploit current and future market opportunities while concurrently minimizing the potential for competitors to affect financial performance. The overall corporate strategy of an organization should be reflected in the company's product range and, in turn, the product strategy should be the determinant of all other elements in the marketing mix (Fig. 7.1).

Given the importance of ensuring that marketing strategies and policies should fulfil the interrelationships illustrated in Fig. 7.1, marketeers must test

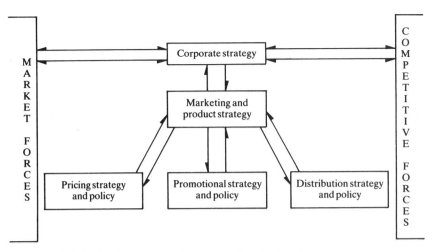

Figure 7.1 Relationship between overall strategy and marketing mix.

any proposed revision in the marketing mix against the two key decision rules of:

- Is the action *consistent* with corporate and product strategy?
- Can the impact on corporate performance be *measured*?

When compatibility and measurability are present, it is likely that the proposed action will (*a*) fulfil the overall corporate strategy, (*b*) be an appropriate response to forecasted market and/or competitive forces, and (*c*) ensure that organizational objectives will be attained.

PRICING DECISIONS

Pricing is a vital responsibility of the marketing operation because decisions on this issue will have a major impact on revenue and profitability. It is of concern, therefore, to realize that many marketeers consider price as a relatively unimportant issue.[1] Furthermore, there is still widespread acceptance of the cost-orientated approach to pricing, where price is calculated on the basis of cost plus a fixed mark-up for profit (e.g., an engineering company making hydraulic pumps that cost £1000 each sets the profit mark-up at 20 per cent of cost to yield a quoted price of £1200). The reality is that customers, not companies, usually determine price. In setting prices, therefore, the marketeer is rarely in the situation so favoured by economists—namely, the company selects a price that maximizes corporate profit. Instead, consideration must be given to customer and competitor behaviour.

Price is used by customers as a key determinant when assessing their perception of the likely quality of goods to be purchased.[2] High prices are

QUALITY PERCEPTION	PRICE Level: High sensitivity: Low	PRICE Level: Average sensitivity: Average	PRICE Level: Low sensitivity: High
High	PREMIUM PRICE Quality is overt influence in buying decision Competitors' claims based on performance, not price comparison	PENETRATION PRICE Product performance is major factor in purchase decision Opportunity to lower costs over longer term through economy of scale or new technology Risk of competitive pressure necessitates immediate achievement of high share	EXTREME VALUE PRICING Product quality remains a market factor Competitive pressure or company need for rapid sales has caused price to become main marketing mix weapon Acceptance of risk that quality claim is undermined by price Price offering may be short-term
Average	SKIMMING PRICE For either status reason or desire to immediately acquire product, customer willing to pay higher than necessary price Competitors not likely to use price as a tactical weapon	AVERAGE PRICE Product quality adequate for majority of customer needs in market High level of competition but based on product differentiation and/or promotional spending Price as long as 'reasonable' is a secondary issue in purchase decision	VALUE PRICE Strong price-based competitive pressures Product performance is a secondary issue
Low	SINGLE SALE PRICING Single purchase or very short duration PLC Competitors either few and/or not use price as tactical weapon	LIMITED REPEAT PRICING Customer in market for limited period Competition not based on price and/or customer not well-informed on price offerings	ECONOMY PRICING Customer's personal values cause price to be dominant purchase factor Strong price-based competition

Figure 7.2 Quality/market conditions pricing strategy matrix.

typically indicative of high quality, and as price declines, the customer usually presumes that this is accompanied by a reduction in quality. An exception to this rule is where the customer comprehends that economy of

PRICE (= Interest and/or service charges)

		High	Average	Low
PERCEIVED QUALITY	High	**PREMIUM PRICE** Fixed charge high personalized service accounts offered by High Street banks to upper income customer groups	**PENETRATION PRICE** Automated card-based transaction systems where in early period of lifecycle price is lower than operating costs in order to stimulate heavy adoption eventually leading to economies of scale	**EXTREME VALUE PRICING** Domestic mortgages offered by overseas lending sources at rates lower than traditional UK sources because of short-term sterling international interest rate imbalances
	Average	**SKIMMING PRICE** Certain status credit/ charge cards made available as a 'company perk' to select groups of employees	**AVERAGE PRICING** Standard current account, overdraft and credit card facilities offered by High Street banks	**VALUE PRICING** Zero interest loan facilities on goods purchased in retail outlets
	Low	**SINGLE PURCHASE PRICING** Finance company 'immediate approval' loans to borrowers with limited or poor credit history	**LIMITED REPEAT PRICING** Charge accounts with high borrowing limits made available to customers by some retail outlets	**ECONOMY PRICING** Current account/loan facilities offered to college students by High Street banks

Figure 7.3 Illustration of pricing strategies adopted by sectors of the UK retail financial services market.

scale (e.g., battery-raised chickens) or new technology (e.g., colour photocopiers) are justification for offering the same quality at a lower price. Hence, in setting or revising prices, the marketeer must give consideration to the desired quality position for company products, because this will influence customers' acceptance of any performance claims based on quality.

In conjunction with the perceived quality issue, the marketeer must also accommodate the behaviour of competition when determining prices. Even the presence of only one or two competitors will usually force the company to reduce prices.[3] In circumstances of extreme competition (e.g., within an industry where there is significant excess capacity) and/or in which the customer is very cost sensitive, the price may become the single most important factor in the purchase decision process.

The combined effect of interactions between perceived quality, competitive behaviour and customer price sensitivity can be incorporated into a pricing strategy matrix of the type illustrated in Fig. 7.2. An application of this matrix in the UK retail financial services sector is shown in Fig. 7.3. In this example, price is paid by the customer in the form of interest and/or account service charges. Quality is perceived by the customer in terms of efficiency of the transaction and/or personal service level of the provider organization.

MONITORING THE VALIDITY OF THE PRICE DECISION

For most products it is feasible to survey customer propensity to buy across a range of prices.[4] The research will typically reveal a bell-shaped price acceptance curve of the type illustrated in Fig. 7.4. Having determined an appropriate product quality/pricing position, marketeers must avoid the dangerous assumption that 'price can now take care of itself', only bestirring themselves to make adjustments when faced with changing industry costs or competitive behaviour.

Customers can be expected to revise their purchase behaviour in response to such factors as experience of the product, changes in their own economic circumstances, the advent of new products and alterations in pricing strategies of other suppliers in the market. If a company has established a market research system that regularly monitors customer attitudes, then any potential shift in buyer behaviour can be identified and an appropriate strategic response formulated. For example, a UK hotel chain may encounter the situation illustrated in Fig. 7.4 where their target customer group is undergoing an attitude shift. Part of the population is tending to favour lower cost facilities and another group is apparently seeking a higher quality product. Assuming that this attitude shift reflects a change in customer disposable income, the hotel may need to consider how to offer existing services at a lower cost or to improve the facilities and reposition the hotel chain in the upper end of the market.

In conjunction with creating a market research system to monitor customer attitudes, the marketing department should continually undertake tests of alternative quality/price scenarios. This will then place the company in a more informed situation should it be necessary to revise pricing strategies because of changing market conditions or competitors' pricing policies. Without this in-depth understanding of the business environment, there is a tendency for marketing departments to either do nothing or panic and drastically reduce prices in the face of a sudden decline in company sales.

SALES PROMOTION—A TACTICAL PRICING STRATEGY

In many consumer goods markets, especially where distribution channels are dominated by a small number of intermediaries, there is a growing tendency to allocate the majority of the marketing budget to funding sales promotions (e.g., price packs, free goods, premiums and competitions).[5] Marketeers will often argue that sales promotions are an important tool in the promotional

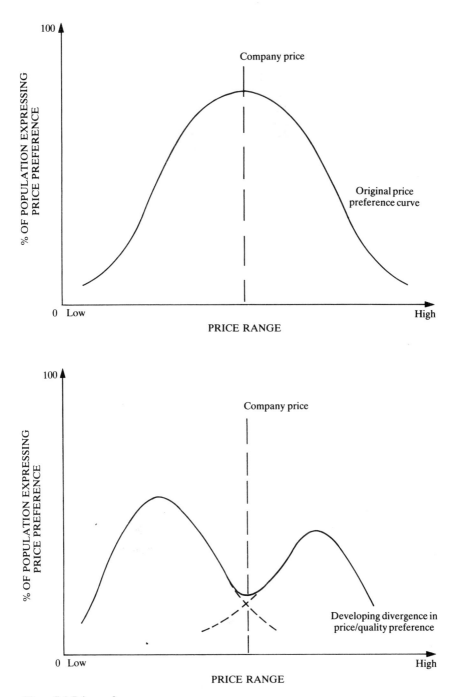

Figure 7.4 Price preference curves.

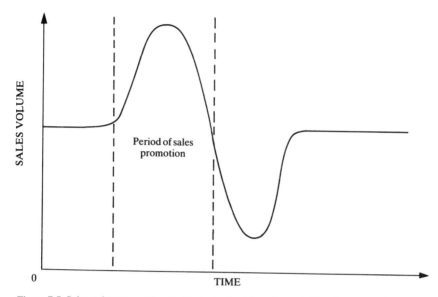

Figure 7.5 Sales volume over time to illustrate short-term impact of a sales promotion.

mix. Unfortunately they rarely endeavour to ensure that sales promotions are consistent with overall product policy or represent an optimal utilization of corporate resources.[6] In terms of consistency with product policy, it should be understood that the majority of sales promotions are perceived by the customer as a temporary reduction in the price of goods. Thus the same assessment as described in Fig. 7.2 should be applied to ensure that a proposed sales promotion is consistent with the existing quality/price positioning strategy.

Just as importantly, it has shown that most sales promotions are tactical in nature and have very little impact on sales volume over the longer term.[7] As demonstrated in Fig. 7.5, what usually occurs is that sales merely increase during the promotional period as customers advance the timing of their purchase to exploit the temporary reduction in price.

Marketeers could improve the effectiveness of promotional activity by setting objectives and by using test-market or buying-behaviour-tracking surveys to assess the cost/benefit relationships of alternative forms of sales promotion.[7] The adoption of this philosophy is likely to increase the probability that sales promotions are compatible with overall strategy and thereby capable of contributing to long-term corporate performance. Product is then less likely to be given away either in an attempt to buy favours with intermediaries by offering massive discounts on 'price packs' or by offering the final customer excessively high discounts in return for a minimal increase in product purchased.

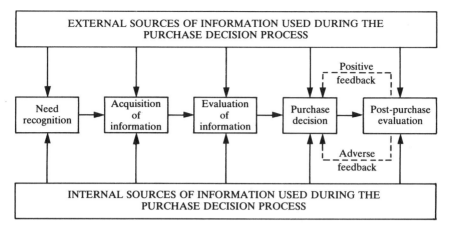

Figure 7.6 Five-stage buyer behaviour model.

PROMOTION—PROCESS AND PLANNING

A simplified illustration of the buyer behaviour process (Fig. 7.6) assumes that the customer moves through five phases during the selection and purchase of a product. To ensure that the most appropriate product is selected, the buyer will seek information from both internal (e.g., experience, views of friends or colleagues) and external sources. The role of the promotional planner is to identify and utilize the most effective techniques to ensure delivery of the required external information. Techniques available to the planner include personal selling, advertising, publicity and corporate collateral materials such as leaflets and brochures.

Research on industry or market specific buyer behaviour will usually reveal a more complicated situation than that illustrated in Fig. 7.6. Examples of actual models which vividly demonstrate the complex nature of the process in consumer markets can be seen in Howard–Sheth[8] and Bettman,[9] and organizational buying situations have been studied by Sheth,[10] Webster–Wind[11] and Choffray–Lilien.[12]

Whichever model a company creates to assist its promotional planning, the four key issues that require understanding in order to optimize the effectiveness of such programmes are:

- Who is the person to whom the information must be addressed (recognizing that, especially in industrial markets, there may be more than one individual seeking information during the purchase decision process)?
- What is the nature of information sought by the customer (e.g., benefit claim for the product, comparison of performance with competition, educational information on the application of new product technology in the customer's environment)?

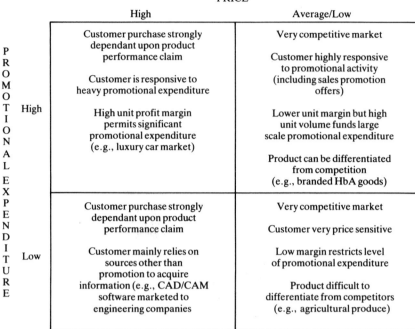

Figure 7.7 Promotion/pricing/market conditions matrix.

- When is the customer in the market seeking information?
- Which promotional channel(s) is (are) likely to be used to acquire the required information?

Having determined the nature, timing and promotional channels used by the customer in the search process, the planner must determine the mix of activities that is both affordable and represents the most cost-effective method of delivering information to the customer. Ultimately the scale of overall promotional spending will be influenced by the market structure and the level of activity by competitors.

Promotional spending in many companies is the single largest area of fund outflow across the entire organization. To be able to afford the activity, therefore, the company will require either a high profit per unit sold, or, where unit profit is lower, a high volume of absolute sales. Where price rather than product performance is the dominant factor in the purchase decision, or where customers seek information from sources other than the supplier's promotional efforts (e.g., recommendations from other members of the same industry), then the level of promotional expenditure will usually be reduced. The interaction of the variables of profit margin and market conditions can be summarized in a matrix of the type illustrated in Fig. 7.7.

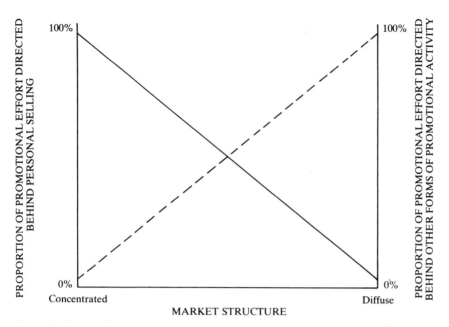

Figure 7.8 Relationship between market structure and importance of personal selling as an element in the promotional mix.

SELECTION OF THE PROMOTIONAL MIX

Personal selling is the most effective method of communication because it permits a two-way dialogue between the company and the customer. The salaries of employees and support costs for a salesforce are very high. Hence, if personal selling is to be cost effective, three key market conditions must prevail:

- There should be very few customers as this will minimize contact and travel costs.
- Each customer must buy significant quantities to recover the high costs of making the individual customer contact.
- The salesperson must be able to gain access to the customer.

In some industrial markets, and in most consumer markets, there are many end-user customers; each end user only buys a limited quantity of product and there may be another level of intermediaries between the supplier and the end user. In these circumstances, the importance of personal selling in the marketing mix will be reduced and other, more cost-effective, promotional methods will be used. Substitution of alternative methods with the aim of optimizing the cost/benefit relationship between expenditure and revenue will be strongly influenced by the nature of the market in which the company is operating. This relationship can be illustrated by a plot of promotional effort against market conditions (Fig. 7.8).

MARKET STRUCTURE

		Concentrated	Diffuse
P R O D U C T	Introduction/ growth phases	*Dominant Promotional Vehicle:* PERSONAL SELLING Few customers needing education and/or training over product application Low level of advertising to stimulate customer enquiries	*Dominant Promotional Vehicle:* ADVERTISING Need to generate product trial/early repeat buyer behaviour Personal selling role to gain support of intermediaries Sales promotion to stimulate trial
L I F E C Y C L E	Maturity/ decline phases	*Dominant Promotional Vehicle:* PERSONAL SELLING Sustain and increase current customer usage, defence against competitive offerings Attract new customers Increasing use of sales promotion and advertising	*Dominant Promotional Vehicle:* ADVERTISING Protect customer base through emphasis of benefit superiority claim Sales promotion can become as important as advertising in mass markets where product differentiation is minimal

Figure 7.9 Market structure/PLC policy matrix.

The promotional mix decision will also be influenced by the PLC. During the introduction/growth phase of market development, the objective will be to generate trial and initial repeat purchase. As the market matures, promotional effort will increasingly focus on sustaining repeat purchase and defending the product against competition. Achievement of this aim may involve communication of performance superiority, repositioning via market segmentation and/or the launch of additional items to expand the breadth of the product range. The influence of the PLC, market structure and selection of promotional mix is summarized in Fig. 7.9.

DISTRIBUTION DECISIONS

Companies often select channels of distribution on the basis of those favoured by the rest of the industry. Marketeers may then assume that the salesforce can be left to contact the appropriate intermediaries and/or end-user customers. This attitude may be dangerously simplistic because it fails to ensure consistency between the overall marketing strategy and the organization's distribution policies.

Two important factors influencing distribution decisions are the degree of control over the market system desired by the company and the current

PRODUCT POSITIONING

		Mass market	Specialist (niche) market
D I S T R I B U T I O N C H A N N E L S	Mass market	Maximize availability of product in marketplace by using all available outlet types (e.g., canned soups in supermarkets, department store food halls, small corner shops)	Specialist product appeal means restriction of product availability to select groups of intermediaries. Often the situation for premium quality goods in consumer markets (e.g., expensive cosmetics)
	Selective	Product is in introduction/early growth stage and hence distribution limited to innovative intermediaries (e.g., satellite receiving systems for television sets) OR Product is in decline and uses outlets specializing in sustaining sales (e.g., discount stores)	Complex nature of product demands intermediaries/agents trained in company product knowledge or company has own direct selling operation (e.g., radar systems for airline industry) OR Market demand does not justify more than one intermediary per sales area

Figure 7.10 Product positioning/distribution policy matrix.

product positioning strategy. A company may feel that a direct channel linking it with the ultimate buyer is necessary. The basis for this opinion may be related to product quality (e.g., dairy producers distributing fresh milk to households by operating their own milk rounds) or because the product requires a significant level of personal contact with the customer (e.g., a manufacturer of specialist earth-moving equipment selling direct to the construction industry).

The selection of an indirect channel will involve distributing product through one or more levels of intermediaries. In many cases the company will select indirect channels because this reduces the total transaction costs of supplying the ultimate purchaser (e.g., a paper mill which produces computer paper for use with laser printers, and which markets its goods through national and regional office supply companies).[13]

Where a company's products are positioned in a specialist market sector, it is probable that only a small number of intermediaries will be needed to achieve the specified sales target. Conversely, a producer of mass market goods (e.g., a range of smoked meats) will probably wish to gain distribution across all channels in both the retail and catering sectors of the food industry. Breadth of market coverage for product positioning strategies will also be influenced by the PLC. The interaction of positioning and the PLC is summarized in Fig. 7.10.

MANAGING THE DISTRIBUTION PROCESS

Having determined an appropriate distribution strategy, the company should create a system to monitor performance across market channels.[15, 16] One fact which might be measured is actual sales rate by outlet type compared to the forecasted sales target. If, for example, a company sales objective for the year is £1 000 000 and there are four intermediaries of similar size in the market channel, the sales per account should be running at a rate approaching £250 000 per year per account. The company order-entry system can provide virtually instant information on sales rates. Yet in many companies little effort is made to evaluate the sales rate by account on a regular basis. Consequently, the first recognition of a developing problem is when one or more intermediaries discontinue the company products on the grounds of an inadequate rate of sale.

The level of availability for a product in the marketplace will significantly influence total sales. Hence, companies should also monitor the percentage of accounts carrying its products relative to a predefined objective. Large consumer goods companies that use advertising as the key form of promotion usually demand that at least 65 per cent of all outlets are carrying the product prior to authorizing expenditure on advertising. Given the critical need for an adequate distribution base, these companies often purchase syndicated panel data from market research organizations such as A. C. Nielsen. These syndicated services will also provide information on the level of 'out-of-stocks', i.e., the proportion of stores which, although authorized to carry product, do not have stocks because their order was insufficient to meet total market demand.

For those companies that operate in market sectors where there are no syndicated services, it is advisable to create their own monitoring system. This can be done by requiring the salesforce to survey intermediaries and identify any distribution problems in key market sectors for both company and competitors' products. Even more effective management of distribution channels can be achieved if the company creates information exchange systems with key customers. This will develop a closer working relationship with channel members, and the point may be reached where the links are a physical barrier to entry by competition.[15]

Another potential risk in placing insufficient priority on distribution management is that opportunities to exploit market gaps may be missed. A classic example of how a company reaped the benefits of understanding the behaviour of intermediaries is the Haines Corporation in America. This company, manufacturing women's tights, realized that intermediaries had great difficulty matching the variety of stock held with actual customer demand. Many retailers had excessive stocks of slow-moving sizes or colours, while frequently being out-of-stock of the most popular lines. Haines developed 'universal' tights that only required three sizes—small, medium and large—to fit any shape of leg. They packaged the product in an egg-shaped container, which in turn racked into a larger 'egg dispenser' for in-store display, and launched it under the clever brand name of L'Eggs. To complete the distribution management process, the company dropped the traditional wholesaler/retailer channel and introduced a rack jobbing service which delivered product direct to end-user outlets. These sales staff could immediately identify any stock imbalances on the display units, remove slow-moving items and expand the stocking level for the faster moving sizes or colours. This effective solution of the distribution problem permitted the company to move to an overwhelmingly dominant market position. The case demonstrates that managing distribution channels is an important facet of the marketeer's responsibilities which, in certain circumstances, can provide an opportunity to gain a significant advantage over competition.

MARKETING MIX ASSESSMENT

Some marketeers prefer intuitive judgement over quantitative decision models when considering alternative choices of marketing mix. This attitude is very prevalent in the area of promotional expenditure, where the marketeer will use justifications such as 'promotions contain an immeasurable creativity element' when questioned by senior management about the potential effectiveness of proposed promotional programmes.

Over the last ten years, however, the large multinationals have invested significant resources in techniques to measure the interaction between those elements that comprise the marketing mix. These organizations have realized that plans based on 'spending set at a fixed proportion of sales' or 'matching the activity of competition' is no longer an acceptable approach when seeking to optimize performance within their marketing operation.

It has not proved easy to develop marketing planning decision models and the complexities of the process are further discussed in the following chapters. Nevertheless, it has now been demonstrated that data on the relationship between promotional activity and sales can be used to construct econometric models. Having created these models, they can be used to examine alternative planning scenarios and thereby permit selection of the plan most likely to optimize future performance.

A classic example of this approach was demonstrated by the Kelloggs company in the early eighties during the UK launch of their Super Noodles product.[16] The company strategy was to attempt entry into an area of the food business outside the breakfast cereals market. It was determined that the strategy should be to remain within the carbohydrate sector, and the new product was to be positioned as a main meal alternative to potatoes. Year 1 targets for awareness (45 per cent of the population) and trial (9 per cent of the population) provided the basis for the promotional budget with the main area of expenditure being on television advertising. Actual results were monitored throughout the year and the data used by the advertising agency Leo Burnett to develop values for their econometric model which expressed sales in terms of:

$$\text{Sales} = a(\text{Adstock}) + b(\text{Retail Level Distribution}) + c(\text{Price}) + d$$

where a, b and c are calculated equation coefficients, d is the intercept on the dependent variables sales axis and 'Adstock' is the weight of advertising expenditure.

Although the objectives for awareness and trial were achieved, the model proved that advertising was an excessively dominant influence on customer purchase behaviour and that housewives still perceived Super Noodles as an impulse purchase product. The Kelloggs company wished to establish a product that was a regular element in the menu cycle of B, C1 and C2 housewives. Further research indicated the need to increase product variety in the Super Noodles range and to improve in-store impact by redesigning the packaging. At the same time the advertising strategy was revised to position Super Noodles as a main meal accompaniment in its own right, not merely an alternative to potatoes.

Using the model to analyse performance and consumer data at the end of Year 2, it was demonstrated that the objective of moving Super Noodles from an impulse to a regularly purchased product had been achieved. It can be concluded from examples such as the Super Noodles case that decision models can assist the marketeer to manage more effectively the marketing mix planning and implementation process.

REFERENCES

1. J. G. Udell, 'How important is pricing in competitive strategy?' *Journal of Marketing*, January 1964.
2. E. B. Ross, 'Making money with proactive pricing', *Harvard Business Review*, November 1984.
3. D. N. Burt and J. E. Boyett Jr, 'Reduction in selling price after the introduction of competition', *Journal of Marketing Research*, vol. 16, May 1979.
4. A. Gabor, *Pricing: Principles and Practice*, Heinemann, 1977.
5. R. Edel, 'Trade wars threaten future peace of marketeers', *Advertising Age*, August 1985.
6. J. A. Quelch, 'It's time to make sales promotions more productive', *Harvard Business Review*, vol. 61, May 1983.
7. M. Christopher, *Marketing Below Line*, Allen & Unwin, 1972.
8. J. A. Howard and J. N. Sheth, *The Theory of Buyer Behaviour*, Wiley, 1969.
9. J. R. Bettman, *An Information Processing Theory of Consumer Choice*, Addison-Wesley, 1979.
10. J. N. Sheth, 'A model of industrial buyer behaviour', *Journal of Marketing*, vol. 37, October 1973.

11. F. E. Webster and Y. Wind, *Organizational Buying Behaviour*, Prentice-Hall, 1972.
12. J. M. Choffray and G. L. Lilien, *Market Planning for New Industrial Products*, Wiley, 1980.
13. R. D. Michmann, 'Marketing channels: a strategic planning approach', *Managerial Planning*, November 1983.
14. P. R. Dickson, 'Distributor portfolio analysis and channel dependence matrix: new techniques for understanding and managing the channel', *Journal of Marketing*, vol. 47, 1983.
15. G. L. Frazier and J. O. Summers, 'Interfirm influence strategies and their application within distribution channels', *Journal of Marketing*, vol. 48, 1984.
16. P. Croome and J. Horsfall, *Key to Success of Super Noodles*, J. J. D. Bullmore (ed.), Advertising Association Handbook, 1983.

EIGHT

FORECASTING AND ASSESSING PERFORMANCE

ADEQUACY OF ANALYSIS

Examination of the annual marketing plans even for large organizations may reveal that the main focus of the submission is concerned with management of the product portfolio and proposed promotional campaigns. In contrast, analysis of current performance versus budget and the rationale behind the recommended sales forecast may receive only a very brief mention.

This situation would be of little concern if today's marketeers were known to be significantly more competent at forecasting than their predecessors in the fifties and sixties. Given the availability of increasingly sophisticated forecasting tools and the very powerful, data processing capability of even personal computers, accuracy of forecasts should now be much higher than in the past. Research evidence tends to suggest, however, that a growing number of companies are facing financial misfortune owing to their continuing inadequacy in accurately forecasting future performance.[1] This trend can only be reversed by marketeers placing greater emphasis on improving the accuracy of forecasts upon which their marketing plans are based. Furthermore, to reassure themselves that this has been achieved, senior management should demand that all plans contain detailed explanations of (a) the factors that are expected to influence performance, (b) why specific performance goals have been proposed, (c) how the forecast compares with prior years and (d) the relationship between sales revenue and the forecasts for operating expense and profitability.

FORECASTING SALES

There are two main types of forecasting technique: subjective predictions based on intuition, and formalized quantitative models involving some form of statistical analysis.[2] Recent research on forecasting methods in US companies revealed that subjective predictions are the most commonly used, followed in importance by the simpler types of quantitative model such as averaging and straight line projections.[3]

In selecting the most appropriate technique, the manager must balance the two factors of accuracy and cost. Forecasts based on personal intuition can be generated at minimal cost. Unfortunately, accuracy will also be low because it is difficult to avoid the influence of expectation or prejudice causing bias in the prediction (e.g., acceptance of an excessively optimistic forecast that is based upon the collective opinions of an enthusiastic salesforce).

Selection of an appropriate statistical method will be greatly influenced by the forecaster's mathematical skills. Marketeers tend to use very basic techniques such as a simple moving average time series which assumes that future demand is directly related to previous sales performance, i.e.:

$$SF_{t+1} = \frac{S_t + S_{t-1} \ldots S_{t-(N-1)}}{N} \qquad (8.1)$$

where SF_{t+1} is the sales forecast for the next period, S_t the current sales, S_{t-1} the sales in a prior time period, $S_{t-(N-1)}$ the sales in the earliest period for which data are available and N the total number of time periods.

The obvious weakness of this method is that it assumes market size and company sales will remain directly proportional to performance in previous years. Even in the increasingly rare situation of a completely stable market, the method still suffers from the weakness of equally weighting sales from all previous periods. In general, future demand is more likely to be influenced by performance in the most recent periods. The marketeer can reflect this effect in the forecast in a relatively simple way by the use of exponential smoothing. This permits sales in the most recent time periods to be weighted more heavily and the weight placed on older time periods to be exponentially decayed. The generalized form for a first-order exponential smoothing equation is:

$$SF_{t+1} = \alpha \, S_t + (1 - \alpha) \, F_t \qquad (8.2)$$

where SF_{t+1} is the sales forecast for the next period, S_t the actual sales in the current period, F_t the forecasted demand in the current period and α the exponential smoothing constant.

For many industrial products, company sales will be strongly influenced by long-term patterns and cyclical economic factors. In these circumstances the marketeer is advised to use some form of time series decomposition

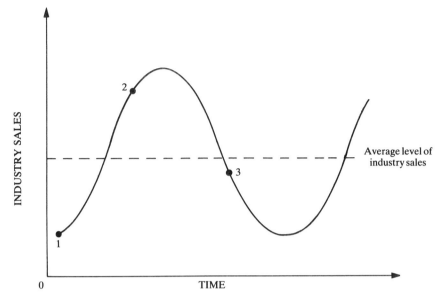

Figure 8.1 Cyclical industry sales situation.

forecasting technique to incorporate relative influence of trends, seasonality and cycles in the predictions of future performance.

Another statistical approach available to the forecaster is that of a causal model where sales are expressed as a function of one or more independent variables (e.g., price, promotional expenditure and competitive pressures). Regression has been identified as the causal method with which users of forecasts are most satisfied.[3] This is due in part to the capability of simple and multiple regression equations to be used in developing 'what if' scenarios during the planning process; for example, by manipulation of values for variables in the equation:

$$S_{t+1} = a + bX_1 + cX_2 + dX_3 + eX_4 \qquad (18.3)$$

where S_{t+1} is the forecasted sales, a, b, c, d and e are regression coefficients, X_1 the advertising expenditure, X_2 the price, X_3 the size of the salesforce and X_4 the sales promotion expenditure.

Further understanding of the influence of various independent variables may be obtained by the construction of an econometric model. This technique uses a set of simultaneous linear equations, typically involving systems of multiple regressions, to predict values for each dependent variable.[4] In those industries that are traditionally very cyclical in nature (e.g., steel, shipbuilding and construction) econometric techniques or forecasts based on lead indicators can be extremely useful in determining both future sales and consequent marketing policies.

As illustrated in Fig. 8.1, a company that has not developed some form of predictive causal model and relies instead on a straight line extrapolation of current year performance, may make a number of mistakes depending upon the status of the industry in the business cycle. At point 1, the company would assume no change in market size and miss the opportunity to exploit the incremental sales available as the market begins to expand. The company at point 2 would assume a continuation of prior year trends and, therefore, invest in further market expansion even though sales are about to enter a decline phase. If consistent logic prevails, at point 3 the company will correctly plan to further reduce marketing effort in the face of a shrinking market. The company may then begin to use its personal judgement, and its optimistic marketing department may decide that the decline phase is almost over and prematurely recommend an expansion in promotional effort.

NEW PRODUCTS

Given the importance of determining the potential for a new product prior to making the significant investment associated with market introduction, major efforts have been expended on developing effective new product forecasting models. One of the most influential advances in this area was achieved by Parfitt and Collins[5] who developed a predictive model in which ultimate market share is based on a function of penetration (i.e., the ultimate percentage of the population who try the product), repeat purchase (i.e., the ultimate proportion of triers who adopt the product) and average usage rate. Later models such as *Tracker*[6] and *Assessor*[7] have further evolved the concept to enhance forecasting accuracy.

If a company is first into a market with a new product, early sales will occur in a virtual monopoly situation. Should the marketeer then use this sales history to predict future performance, the analysis may not take into consideration the potential impact of other similar products entering the market at a slightly later date. This scenario appears to have occurred among certain companies who were early entrants into the UK personal computer market. Having achieved very high sales in their early years, a euphoria seemed to develop which stimulated investment in significant expansion in production capacity. As new competitors were attracted to the market (often offering improved technology at the same price) a number of companies were unable to sustain historic sales trends and were forced into a period of financial difficulty by their ownership of expensive, but now underutilized, manufacturing facilities.

Thus, another factor that should be considered in the forecasting process is the influence of the PLC on future performance. It must be recognized, however, that differences in cycle length and the varying influence of external variables (e.g., economic conditions, market structure, buyer behaviour) can combine to reduce significantly the accuracy of predictions concerning the impact of the lifecycle on future sales.[8] Nevertheless, companies should require that their marketing departments continue to sustain the intensity of market research used in test market situations to monitor trial and repeat purchase patterns throughout the life of the product. These data can then provide early indications of any downturn in product performance that might occur in the event of a new competitive entry or a revision in the marketing mix by an existing company in the market.

MANAGING THE FUTURE

The above discussions assume that companies have sufficient history of performance from which to extrapolate an accurate forecast of future performance. In some industries, especially those involving the development and application of new technologies (e.g., information technology, defence equipment, aerospace and pharmaceuticals), it is often the case that market conditions alter dramatically in a short space of time. In such cases, neither subjective predictions based on experience nor statistical models are likely to provide the company with any meaningful forecast of future opportunity. In recognition of this, a number of research groups and planners within high technology companies have begun to develop qualitative and technological approaches to forecast performance in circumstances of high uncertainty and/or extremely limited existing information.

Many statistical methods attempt to identify a trend and extend this into the future. Such techniques are rendered useless where a new technology has dramatic impact on buyer behaviour (e.g., the effect of television on the growth of sales for radios). Hence a key objective of qualitative and technological forecasting techniques is to identify possible interrelationships between scientific discovery and incorporation of new knowledge into the development of future products. One technique of this type is the Morphological method created by the Swiss astronomer Zwicky in which the user develops a checklist to determine, systematically, new combinations of technological possibility.[9] An even more well-known technique, the Delphi method, also attempts to examine interactions of numerous variables but relies upon the use of a broad range of inputs from a specially convened panel of experts. A recently developed extension of the Delphi technique is the Cross-Impact method.[10] In this technique, events predicted by a Delphi-type review are assigned probabilities that can be used in developing scenarios to show the most likely outcome of changes in technological and/or socio-economic conditions.

Advocates of another approach known as 'Futuribles' or 'La Prospective' have argued that many of the qualitative and technological methods are impaired by the preconceptions and experience of the forecaster. To overcome this potential bias, the 'futuribles' approach assumes that the future contains numerous alternatives and uncertainties. Multiple scenarios are constructed and analysed to identify paths or factors that would have a strong influence over such events should they ever occur.[11]

ENHANCED ACCURACY

For those companies who decide that there is a need to enhance the accuracy of their forecasting system, there are two issues to be considered. These are (a) selecting the most appropriate method(s) and (b) creating an internal climate which emphasizes the importance of accurate performance prediction in influencing the future destiny of the organization. The starting point for the selection of method is to define clearly the time span for the forecasts (i.e., short range, intermediate or long range) and the desired level of accuracy. The more rigorous, sophisticated techniques tend to result in a higher level of accuracy, but they are usually also costly in terms of investment in computer hardware and/or software, maintenance of large data bases and ongoing computer operating costs. Management should select systems that provide an optimal balance between costs and the value to the company of achieving a specified level of forecasting accuracy.[12]

Research on the managerial problems associated with the operation of forecasting systems has revealed a number of issues that will be addressed.[13] The psychology of the average manager is to favour the use of methods with which he is already familiar. Because of this, care should be taken not to adopt techniques simply because they are ones with which the marketing staff feel most comfortable.

Within the marketing operation, forecasting is usually delegated to a junior member of the management team. There must be, therefore, a clearly articulated company policy about the performance of the individual as a forecaster and their future promotional prospects in this role, for without this, individuals will see no benefit in developing the necessary technical skills because their current position will be perceived as a short-term stepping stone to greater things within the organization. Having established the vital status of the forecasting role, senior management should then confirm this policy by ensuring that sufficient ongoing investment is made in continuing the expansion of data bases and the introduction of new advances in systems technology.

MARKETING EXPENDITURE

Managers from most departments in an organization, when seeking approval for planned expenditures, are usually required to submit a detailed analysis

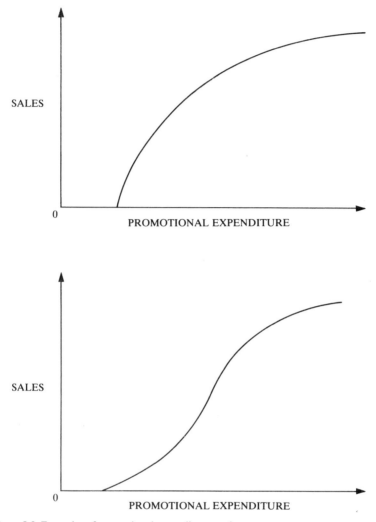

Figure 8.2 Examples of promotional expenditure – sales response curves.

in support of their proposals (e.g., cost/benefit review, three-year cash flow, discounted cash flow or interval rate of return calculation). In contrast, some marketing plans contain only a very brief mention of the rationale behind proposed expenditures. Furthermore, recommendations appear to be approved by senior management after only a very cursory review.

Marketing budgets, especially in organizations that operate in highly competitive consumer goods or service sectors, often represent the largest single cash outflow for the company. Given the ease with which these budgets are approved, one can only hypothesize that senior management have assumed the marketing department proposals to be based on extensive, detailed market research. The reality, however, is that marketing budgets are often calculated using very basic techniques.[14] One common approach is to set expenditure at a specified percentage of sales. Another related approach—comparative parity—is based upon the philosophy of setting spending at the same level as that of competition. Finally, there are marketeers who set the budget on the basis of what they think the company can afford (or, put another way, the expenditure the marketeer feels senior management will accept without any further debate).

In defence of these crude methods, there is some validity in this rendering of a famous quotation. 'We know that 50 per cent of our marketing spending is effective, the only problem is we don't know which 50 per cent.' This reflects the influences of interactions between the marketing mix and changes in market conditions that the market researcher will face in attempting to specify any relationship between performance and expenditure. Nevertheless, sufficient empirical evidence now exists to substantiate the view that this relationship is either S-shaped or one of diminishing returns (Fig. 8.2).[15]

In those organizations where, currently, no real analysis is undertaken prior to determining marketing expenditure, it is unrealistic to expect that overnight the marketing group could install a sophisticated system of predictive planning models. Within virtually all companies, however, data exist which permit some fundamental questions being posed over alternative spending strategies. For example, the hypothetical company in Table 8.1 faces variation in gross profit across the product line, but is currently allocating promotional funds in direct relation to sales volume. Thus it is not unreasonable to consider the implications of changing to set promotional spending in direct proportion to gross profit. The forecasted outcome is that sales remain virtually unchanged, but overall profitability would be significantly enhanced.

Another useful form of cost/benefit analysis is to compare the company expenditure:sales ratio with competition. As shown in Table 8.2, a hypothetical company is proposing to sustain marketing expenditure at a funding rate of 8 per cent of sales. Yet a comparison with other organizations reveals that (a) Competitor A has a similar rate of sales growth but has reduced absolute expenditure and (b) Competitor B is achieving a faster sales growth rate at a funding level of only 6 per cent of sales.

With this additional knowledge, any future marketing plan should focus on the opportunity either to sustain the current rate of sales at a lower level of promotional spending or, if promotional support is to remain at 8 per cent of sales, to demand an improvement in the future sales growth. Assuming that further research demonstrated that the competitors' achievements are the result of a more effective mix of promotional activity (i.e., price or product performance are not the reason for performance variation), then the company should implement a restructuring of their promotional

Table 8.1 Analysis of an alternative promotional spending strategy

Current strategy of spending in direct proportion to sales volume (£'000)

	Product type			Total
	1	2	3	
Sales	5 000	3 000	2 000	10 000
Gross profit	1 000	750	600	2 350
(Margin %)	(20)	(25)	(30)	(23.5)
Promotional expense	250	150	100	500
(% of sales)	(5)	(5)	(5)	(5)
Net profit	750	600	500	1 850

Forecasted impact of moving to a strategy of allocating promotional funds in direct proportion to gross profit (£'000)

	Product type			Total
	1	2	3	
Forecasted Sales*	4 200	3 210	2 600	10 010
Gross profit	840	820.5	780	2 422.5
(Margin %)	(20)	(25)	(30)	(24.2)
Promotional expense	210	160	130	500
(Change in % of sales)	(− 16)	(+ 7)	(+ 30)	(+ 0.1)
Net profit	630	660.5	650	1 940.5
Change in net profit vs scenario above	− 120	+ 60.5	+ 150	+ 90.5

* Forecast assumes that sales will alter in direct proportion to change in level of promotional spending by product category.

programmes for the coming year. Should the marketing department believe this to be an excessively risky decision, then at minimum a series of promotional spending tests should be scheduled. These will result in a better understanding of the relationship between alternative promotional methods and company sales.

MODEL BUILDING AND THE PLANNING PROCESS

Having established within the organization the benefits of making a detailed analysis of information contained within the management accounting system, the next step is for more marketeers to introduce computer-based models to further examine the relationship between promotional spending

Table 8.2 Analysis of company and key competitor performance

Company forecast for next 12 months

Sales	5 250
Promotion	420
Promotion (as % of sales)	8

Company performance over latest 3 years vs competition

	Prior-prior year	Prior year	Current year
Company sales	4 800 (100)	4 900 (102)	5 000 (104)
Promotional expense	384	392	400
Promotion (as % of sales)	8	8	8
Competitor A sales	6 600 (100)	6 800 (103)	7 000 (106)
Promotional expense	540	530	525
Promotion (as % of sales)	8.2	7.8	7.5
Competitor B sales	2 000 (100)	2 400 (120)	2 800 (140)
Promotional expense	120	144	168
Promotion (as % of sales)	6.0	6.0	6.0

and performance. Such models offer the potential to enhance significantly the abilities of the marketing department to develop plans that can optimize performance. The concept of planning by model building has, however, gained only limited acceptance in the world of marketing. This situation has arisen because (*a*) some managers are still averse to using computers as an aid to decision-making and (*b*) the complex interactions between the variables in the marketing mix does mean that development of effective models is no easy task.[16]

To assist in the management of a salesforce, most companies now regularly gather information on numbers and types of customer, call frequencies, duration of sales call and order size. By analysing this rich source of data, researchers have been able to establish clear statistical relationships between sales volume and the variables of customer size, time spent with customers and call frequency. Hence, the personal selling process was the first area selected by both academics and company operations researchers when they wanted to create models that could be used in simulations of alternative promotional spending strategies. Following the success of models such as CALLPLAN,[17] a number of commercial software packages are available to the marketeer who seeks to select the best cost/benefit proposition from a number of alternative salesforce expenditure plans.

Telesales is now proving to be one of the most cost-effective promotional tools available to the marketeer. This has occurred because companies introduced computer-based information systems to provide sales staff with more rapid access to customer files. With field sales systems there is a time lag between action, data collection and collation, whereas in a telesales operation staff are directly linked to the company data-processing facility and the impact of their activities can be assessed instantly. It was soon realized that with only minor modifications, existing field salesforce decision models can become an extremely powerful tool for assessing alternative expenditure plans for a telesales operation. The ease with which these systems can be installed, and their benefits immediately demonstrated, has meant that telesales is now the area in which there is greatest acceptance of the concept of using model building to optimize future promotional programmes.

Advertising and sales promotion planning models which attempt to reflect all of the theoretical aspects of the promotional process have proved much more difficult to develop. Little,[15] for example, has recommended that an effective a priori advertising response model should incorporate the following items:

- Sales responding dynamically upward or downward will reflect increases and decreases in advertising expenditure.
- Steady-state sales response will be concave or S-shaped and will often exhibit positive sales at zero advertising activity.
- Competitive activity will affect sales.
- Cost effectiveness of a campaign will vary over time as the result of changes in media channels, creative execution and other related factors.
- Products will respond to increased expenditure, but sales may also decline even though advertising spending is held constant.

In the face of these theoretical complexities, many market researchers have been forced to adopt a pragmatic approach to model building. As a result they have created simulations to reflect observed market conditions, but have incorporated few of the known theories of the promotion process. Nevertheless, progress is being made to overcome the problems of combining both reality and theory into the modelling process (e.g., the BRANDAID aggregate marketing model created by Little[18]). It seems likely, therefore, that commercial advertising and sales promotion decision-making software that utilizes a priori concepts will be available to the marketing practitioner within the foreseeable future.

BALANCE SHEET PERFORMANCE

It is common practice in many organizations that, after the marketing group has generated a sales and profit forecast, the accountancy department will use these data to prepare a balance sheet and calculate ROI. If their calculations reveal an inadequate performance relative to corporate goals, then the marketing department will be asked to re-examine their forecast to see if ROI can be improved by increasing the sales of gross margin forecast and/or decreasing the level of planned expenditure.

It is not surprising in these circumstances to find that some marketeers perceive balance sheets and ROI as somewhat unimportant as the concerns of senior management can readily be placated by merely massaging perform-ance or expenditure forecasts. This perspective is, of course, fallacious because mistakes that affect the profit and loss statement can often be remedied by revisions to the marketing mix in subsequent years. In contrast, planning errors, which weaken the balance sheet, may ultimately lead to the demise of the organization. This situation can be illustrated by examining the fund flows associated with the launch of a new product. Manufacturing capacity has to be expanded and this will involve borrowing via long-term loans, the issuance of additional shares and/or drawing upon corporate profit reserves. As the launch date approaches, levels of finished goods, work-in-progress and creditor balances will begin to rise. Once sales occur, debtor balances will increase and, to fund the resultant cash shortage, short-term borrowing may be necessary.

If actual sales are significantly less than forecasted, the levels of finished goods and work-in-progress, although creating an increase in net current assets (i.e., current assets less liabilities due in under 12 months), may cause lenders to be concerned about liquidity (i.e., the company's ability to raise sufficient cash to satisfy demands from creditors). Concurrently, the new manufacturing facility will be operating at well below capacity. The overall situation may raise questions about the company's ability to meet interest charges and/or loan repayments. Lower than forecasted sales will mean reduced profits and this, when combined with the status of higher asset balances, will mean a decline in ROI. This can make shareholders nervous about the future prospects for dividends and, in the case of public-quoted companies, the share price may fall.

To avoid such scenarios (i.e., a new product failure undermining the continued existence of a company), it is imperative that during the planning process marketeers place emphasis on examining the relationship between sales, profits and the level of net assets needed to implement any new marketing programme. In making this recommendation, however, the mar-keteer must understand that the only acceptable path to achieving corporate ROI objectives is a marketing plan that will further strengthen the company's market position. This point is stressed because some marketeers are willing to enhance ROI by underfunding any activity (e.g., investment in new product development) which represents a near-future drain on profits. Such actions may please shareholders who then enjoy the benefits of an increase in earnings per share; but there is a major risk that myopic actions of this type will, in the long term, erode the company's ability to sustain a strong position

Table 8.3 Company data on current profitability and asset utilization (£'000)

	Product Group				Total
	1	2	3	4	
Sales	750	1 250	2 200	800	5 000
Net profit	150	150	396	120	816
Net current assets*	94	312	733	200	1 339
Fixed assets	441	368	790	228	1 827
Net investment†	535	680	1 523	428	3 166
ROI (%)	28.0	22.0	26.0	28.0	25.8
Manufacturing capacity utilization (%)	60.0	80.0	98.0	70.0	81.0
Prior year ROI (%)	24.0	23.0	26.0	26.0	25.0
Prior-prior year ROI (%)	20.0	24.0	26.0	24.0	24.2

* Calculated from (current assets less liabilities due in under 12 months)
† Sum of net current assets and fixed assets (i.e., equivalent to capital employed).

in the market place. Eventually, of course, shareholder euphoria will be rudely shattered when the increasingly obsolete product line becomes vulnerable to competition from more far-sighted organizations who had not mortgaged their future by cutting back on expensive development projects just to keep their investors happy.

Assessment of future ROI can be achieved during the planning process by analysing the relationship between sales, working capital and fixed assets for each item or group of items in the product line. This approach can be illustrated by using the data in Table 8.3. To aid the ROI assessment, information on manufacturing capacity trends and the age of fixed assets has been provided. Corporate ROI has been marginally improving over the last three years (having risen from 24.2 to 25.8 per cent). With the exception of the recently introduced high margin Product 1, the company's other three products have in the past been provided with promotional support in direct proportion to annual sales volume. A review of the information on ROI, performance trends and manufacturing capacity for the example company in Table 8.3 might lead to the following revisions in marketing policy:

Product 1 generates a high margin and has a low requirement for working capital. The relatively new plant and equipment means there is a high investment in fixed assets as a percentage of sales. Nevertheless, as sales grow, plant capacity utilization is improving and ROI will increase. Consideration should therefore be given to ways of further accelerating sales growth because this offers an ROI in excess of 30 per cent.

Product 2 has a declining ROI because the highly competitive nature of the market over recent years has eroded profitability. Consideration should now be given to moving to a more aggressive pricing policy to stimulate sales.

(It is assumed that the market sector contains a high proportion of price sensitive customers.) Although this action will decrease unit profit margins, the relatively low working capital requirements and the subsequent improvement in utilization of manufacturing capacity should reverse the declining ROI trend.

Product 3 is in a mature market and ROI has remained static over the last three years. The high working capital requirements reflect a manufacturing capacity constraint that causes the company to keep a higher than average finished goods inventory on hand to cover both unexpected sales surges and plant downtime for maintenance of production equipment. To improve the supply/demand situation, consideration should be given to increasing the price. This action will generate a higher unit profit, and the resultant decrease in unit sales will reduce the working capital requirements associated with high inventory requirements. The ROI will then improve as long as the unit profit improvement offered by the price increase is not eroded by any increase in promotional expenditure. Over the longer term, the marketing and production departments should examine whether the potential duration of the maturity phase of the product lifecycle would justify an investment in additional manufacturing capacity.

Product 4 is the oldest item in the product line. The market has entered the decline phase and both sales and profits have been falling. The low working capital requirements, coupled with the fact that plant and equipment values have been almost fully depreciated over the years, means that ROI has been increasing. As there is little future for the product category, promotional funds should be redirected to stimulate sales growth for Product 1. This reduction in promotional effort will increase Product 4 profitability and further improve the ROI.

REFERENCES

1. R. N. Paul, N. B. Donavan and J. W. Taylor, 'The reality gap in strategic planning', *Harvard Business Review*, vol. 56, No. 3, May 1978.
2. R. E. Markland and J. R. Sweigart, *Quantitative Methods: Applications to Managerial Decision-Making*, Wiley, 1987.
3. J. T. Mentzer and J. E. Cox, 'Familiarity, application and performance of sales forecasting techniques', *Journal of Forecasting*, vol. 3, No. 1, 1984.
4. S. Makridakis and S. C. Wheelwright, *Forecasting: Methods and Applications*, Wiley, 1977.
5. J. H. Parfitt and B. J. K. Collins, 'Use of consumer panels for brand share predictions', *Journal of Marketing Research*, vol. 5, May 1968.
6. R. C. Blattberg and J. Golanty, 'Tracker: an early test market forecasting and diagnostic model for new product planning', *Journal of Marketing Research*, vol. 15, May 1978.
7. A. J. Silk and G. L. Urban, 'Pre-test market evaluation of new packaged goods: a model and measurement methodology', *Journal of Marketing Research*, vol. 15, May 1978.
8. D. R. Rink and J. E. Swan, 'Product life cycle research: a literature review', *Journal of Business Research*, vol. 7, No. 3, September 1979.

9. F. Zwicky, *Morphology of Propulsive Power: Monographs on Morphological Research*, No. 1, Society of Morphological Research, Pasadena, CA, 1962.

10. R. Rochberg, T. J. Gordon and O. Helmer, 'The use of cross-impact matrices for forecasting and planning', Report R–10, Institute for the Future, Middletown, CT, April 1970.

11. M. Godet, 'From forecasting to "La Prospective": a new way of looking at futures', *Journal of Forecasting*, vol. 1, No. 3, 1982.

12. J. S. Chambers, S. K. Mullick and D. S. Smith, *Harvard Business Review*, vol. 49, July 1971.

13. S. C. Wheelwright and S. Makridakis, *Forecasting Methods for Managers*, 4th edn, Wiley, 1985.

14. G. L. Lilien and J. D. C. Little, 'The ADVISOR project: a study of industrial marketing budgets', *Sloan Management Review*, vol. 17, No. 3, Spring 1976.

15. J. D. C. Little, 'Aggregate advertising models: the state of the art', *Operations Research*, vol. 27, No. 4, July 1979.

16. G. L. Lilien and P. Kotler, *Marketing Decision-Making: A Model Building Approach*, Harper & Row, 1983.

17. L. M. Lodish, 'CALLPLAN: an interactive salesman's call planning system', *Management Science*, vol. 18, No. 4, Part II, December 1971.

18. J. D. C. Little, 'BRANDAID: a marketing mix model, Part I: Structure; Part II: Implementation' , *Operations Research*, vol. 23, 1975.

NINE

PERFORMANCE CONTROL

FROM INFORMATION TO CONTROL

Management theorists in the sixties and seventies were predicting that, with the advent of the computer, companies would increasingly apply this new, powerful tool to enhance corporate performance by installing information technology (IT) control systems throughout every level of the organization. Although this may have come to pass in very large organizations, research has shown that most companies have been slow to adopt computer-based information systems. Even where such systems are in place, their control capability frequently lacks any degree of sophistication.[1]

A fundamental ethos of the scientist, technologist and manager in the more numerate business disciplines is to avoid instigating an action unless the outcome can be evaluated against a predetermined standard. Those who understand the benefits of performance by control are often surprised to find that many marketeers actively avoid any system that could help them monitor performance versus plan. This difference in attitude explains why, in many companies, the marketeers continue to operate using what they consider to be 'entrepreneurial judgement'—even though other departments use control systems to assist in the management process. Other managers may consider a better description to be 'totally out of control'.

Marketeers' limited acceptance of effective controls frequently leads to senior management being informed of unexpected surprises such as sales or profits being below budget. Even where some form of control mechanism is in place, the ability of the system to be of any benefit is often questionable. This situation prevails because the requirement for a control system has originated with senior management. The marketing department will then design a system that can be operated with minimal effort. In consequence, the

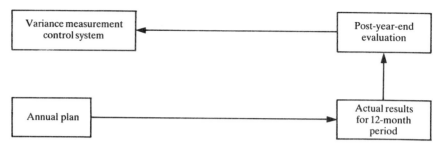

Figure 9.1 Annual plan absolute control system.

information generated will be of limited benefit in enhancing the quality of the decision-making processes within the marketing operation.

LIMITED CONTROL

A common form of non-functional marketing control is to create a system that has no feedback capability. An example of this approach is the absolute control of the type shown in Fig. 9.1. Having established an annual plan objective, no review of actual performance then occurs until twelve months later when the next marketing plan is being prepared. Should a variance between planned and actual performance become apparent, it is too late to instigate any form of response that could improve the current year's performance.

One improvement is the move to a periodic control system where the frequency of performance analysis increases from once a year to every month. The only new element that has to be added to the basic system is a translation of the annual objective into a series of monthly targets (Fig. 9.2). Once a periodic control comparison is in place, the company is given an earlier warning of the potential variance in annual performance. For example, the periodic control system operated by a company manufacturing office furniture revealed the performance variance summarized in Table 9.1.

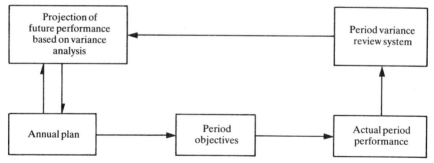

Figure 9.2 Periodic performance control system.

Table 9.1 Forecasts for Office Life Ltd

	Sales (£'000)			
	Annual	Period 1	Period 2	Period 3
Forecast	12 000	500	700	900
Actual	N/A	450	630	810
Variance (%)	N/A	− 10	− 10	− 10

By comparing the variance between actual and forecasted sales, it can be concluded that the monthly revenue is running consistently at 10 per cent lower than budget. It is reasonable to suggest that without an improvement in actual performance in the subsequent months, total sales for the year are likely to be at least £1.3 million lower than planned.

The periodic control approach can also be used to compare actual versus forecasted marketing expenditure. These data will be more informative if the level of expenditure is expressed as a percentage of sales. For example, a first quarter marketing budget from the Office Life Ltd was set at £105 000, yielding budgeted expenditure/sales ratio of 5 per cent. Actual expenditure was £105 000 which, upon initial consideration, appears reasonable because it is £5000 lower than budget. As a percentage of sales, however, actual expenditure is running at 5.3 per cent versus the forecast of 5 per cent. Not only is sales revenue below target, therefore, but the relative cost of generating even this level of sales is higher than budgeted.

DIAGNOSTIC CONTROL

The improvement in the system illustrated in Fig. 9.2 versus that of Fig. 9.1 is of little help if the management objective is to use controls as a mechanism for enhancing the quality of future marketing decisions. Although periodic analysis can provide early warning of developing problems or opportunities, these types of data do not provide any explanation of why a variance from forecast has occurred. To create a control model that can fulfil this objective will require the addition of some form of diagnostic capability, as illustrated in Fig. 9.3.

In creating a diagnostic control system, the marketing department must determine which issues should be given priority in attempting to understand the reasons underlying a variance in performance. Ineffectual forecasting was earlier considered in Chapter 8. Assuming this to be no longer a problem, then the most likely causes external to the company are a change in (a) total market size or (b) the capability of competitors. Predictions about these factors are usually contained within the annual plan. Measurement of actual

Table 9.2 Forecasted and actual first quarter results for Wood Care Ltd

	Total market (£'000)	Company sales (£'000)	Share (%)
Forecast	10 000	2 000	20
Actual	8 000	1 280	16
Variance	2 000	720	− 4
Variance (%)	− 20	− 36	N/A

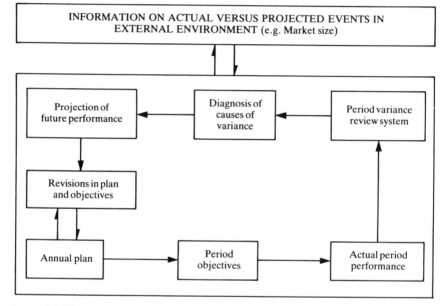

Figure 9.3 Diagnostic control system.

trends in market size or competitive activity will require a market research programme generating data to compare with conditions assumed in the planning phase.

The benefits of a market analysis diagnostic system can be demonstrated by the disguised case of a manufacturer of wood stains—Wood Care Ltd. The forecasted and actual sales for the first quarter are shown in Table 9.2. It can be concluded from these data that of the total £720 000 variance in sales, £400 000 is due to the total market not attaining the size expected. The balance of shortfall in Wood Care sales is explained by the share loss to competition.

When the company originally designed their diagnostic system, they found that their industry was not large enough to attract a market research company prepared to provide syndicated sales and competitive share information. Hence the company marketing group regularly interview their sales personnel, and on a quarterly basis survey major intermediaries, to obtain information on both market size and competitive activity. The data on Wood Care's competitors reveal that there are two organizations who are enjoying very rapid growth in sales. One of these has introduced a new range of 'designer colour' wood stains, which offers customers a much broader choice than that available from Wood Care. The other rapidly growing competitor has been offering a major temporary price reduction promotional allowance for the last two months.

This gives the marketing department the knowledge that the fall in market share is partially caused by a short-term promotional activity by one competitor. As this campaign is now over, that particular competitor is unlikely to have further impact on Wood Care in the second quarter. The launch of the new designer colour stains by the other competitor is, however, liable to affect company performance for the balance of the financial year.

DIAGNOSTIC FINANCIAL VARIANCE CONTROL

Understanding the causes of differences between actual and planned performance can be further enhanced by linking the market analysis diagnostic control to an internal mechanism that breaks sales down into the two variables of unit price and unit volume.[2] This can be achieved by installing a standard cost system and then applying a technique known as variance analysis. Where the company markets a range of products, further understanding of sales performance versus budget can be achieved by variance analysis of individual items in the product line. An illustration of the technique is provided for Wood Care Ltd in Table 9.3.

Gross profit is calculated by deducting cost of goods from sales revenue. Merely to know, for example, that Wood Care achieved an actual gross profit in a quarter of £525 500 versus the forecast of £862 500 is of limited value. Thus in order to diagnose the relative importance of volume versus unit profit variance in the performance shortfall, it would be beneficial to carry out a variance analysis of the type illustrated in Table 9.4.

DIAGNOSTIC MANAGERIAL ACCOUNTING CONTROL

Standard accounting statements such as profit and loss accounts and balance sheets were created for the purpose of recording history in a universally accepted format that could be understood by external bodies (e.g., financial institutions, shareholders and Government tax departments). Unfortunately this philosophy usually results in financial records being produced in a

Table 9.3 An example of variance analysis to determine cause of sales volume versus budget

	First quarter budget		
Product	Sales (£'000)	Sales units ('000)	Price/unit (£)
Product A	990	1500	0.66
Product B	610	500	1.22
Product C	400	250	1.60
Total	2000	2250	N/A

	First quarter actual performance		
Product	Sales (£'000)	Sales units ('000)	Price/unit (£)
Product A	640	1000	0.64
Product B	385	350	1.10
Product C	255	150	1.70
Total	1280	1500	N/A

To calculate volume and price/unit variance, the following equations can be applied:

$$\text{Volume variance} = (\text{Actual units} - \text{Budgeted units}) \times (\text{Actual price per unit})$$

$$\text{Price variance} = (\text{Actual price} - \text{Budget price}) \times (\text{Budgeted units})$$

Applying these equations yields the following:

		Variance (£'000)	% of variance
Product A			
Volume variance = (1000 − 1500) (0.64)	=	− 320	91%
Price variance = (0.64 − 0.66) (1500)	=	− 30	9%
		− 350	100%
Product B			
Volume variance = (350 − 500) (1.10)	=	− 165	73%
Price variance = (1.10 − 1.22) (500)	=	− 60	27%
		− 225	100%
Product C			
Volume variance = (150 − 250) (1.70)	=	− 170	100%
Price variance = (1.70 − 1.60) (250)	=	+ 25	N/A
		− 145	100%

Table 9.4 An example of variance analysis to determine cause of sales volume vs budget

	First quarter budget			
Product	Sales (£'000)	Sales units ('000)	Profit/unit (£)	Total profit (£'000)
Product A	1000	1500	0.25	375
Product B	600	500	0.60	300
Product C	400	250	0.75	187.5
Total	2000	2250	0.383	862.5

	First quarter actual performance			
Product	Sales (£'000)	Sales units ('000)	Profit/unit (£)	Total profit (£'000)
Product A	640	1000	0.23	230
Product B	380	350	0.48	168
Product C	260	150	0.85	127.5
Total	1280	1500	0.350	525.5

To calculate volume and price/unit variance, the following equations can be applied:

Volume variance

= (Actual units − Budgeted units) × (Actual profit per unit)

Unit profit variance

= (Actual profit per unit − Budgeted profit per unit) × (Budgeted units)

Applying these equations to the three product groups yields the following:

				Variance (£'000)	% of variance
Product A					
Volume variance	=	(1000 − 1500)(0.23)	=	− 115	79%
Price variance	=	(0.64 − 0.66)(1500)	=	− 30	21%
				− 145	100%
Product B					
Volume variance	=	(250 − 500)(0.48)	=	− 72	55%
Unit profit variance	=	(0.48 − 0.60)(500)	=	− 60	45%
				− 132	100%
Product C					
Volume variance	=	(150 − 250)(0.80)	=	− 85	100%
Price variance	=	(0.85 − 0.75)(250)	=	+ 25	N/A
				− 60	N/A

consolidated form, which are of little use to a manager seeking to understand the causes of poor financial performance.[3, 4]

The utility of even a simple management accounting diagnostic control system can be illustrated by the disguised case of A. E. Smith Ltd. This company manufactures electrical accessories such as plugs, switches and lighting fixtures. The company was established to exploit the sector of the market that is seeking high modernity designs available in a wide range of colours. Initially the marketing group concentrated on the industrial sector by seeking distribution through builders' merchants. Consumer sales were seen as less important and distribution was restricted to specialist DIY stores who mainly supplied small building companies. The main focus of promotional effort was the salesforce calling on the trade, larger builders and architects. These activities were supplemented by small-scale expenditure on mail shots and trade exhibitions.

After a few years the marketing department decided to expand distribution into retail sector DIY outlets (independent and national chain operations) and to supply own-label items to department store chains. To generate business in the latter sector, a 15 per cent price discount versus Smith brand products was required. Additional sales staff were hired and the promotional support broadened to include advertising in consumer magazines and consumer sales promotion events. The main element of this latter activity was the use of temporary price discounts on selected key items at various times in the year with the aim of stimulating in-store displays of Smith merchandise.

The marketing department were pleased with the results of their new plan, pointing out to management that sales had doubled and profitability had risen by 86 per cent. Feedback from intermediaries was less positive, however, because they found that in-store sales rates per square foot for Smith brand products was much lower than other suppliers. The recommendation of the marketing department was to increase promotional expenditure as a percentage of sales from 5.7 to 8, which would bring the company in line with the expenditure : sales ratio for the industry. They also considered that sales rates on own-label product could be significantly accelerated if prices to the department stores were reduced by a further 5 per cent. This plan was justified (Table 9.5, Section A) on the grounds that the recent improvement in sales was mainly attributable to actions in the retail sector and that this area of business represented the best source of future opportunity.

The Smith situation can be used to illustrate the hazards of basing marketing plans on conclusions drawn from consolidated financial records. By using a management accounting system which breaks down sales and profits into market/product sectors (Table 9.5, Section B) the new areas of business are found to be barely profitable. In addition, the proposed 5 per cent reduction in own-label goods would actually force this segment of business into a loss situation. Finally, should the proposed increase in promotional

Table 9.5 Financial performance of A. E. Smith Ltd

Section A: Consolidated profit and loss accounts (£'000)

	Three years ago	Current year
Sales	5 000	10 000
Cost of goods	2 500	5 300
Gross profit	2 500	4 700
Salesforce expense	250	600
Advertising/exhibitions	80	160
Sales promotion	70	570
General administration	1 350	1 975
Total expense	1 750	3 305
Net profit	750	1 395
Profit as % of sales	15.0	14.0

Section B: Breakdown of current profit by market sector (£'000)

	Builders merchants	Specialist DIY	Chain DIY	Department store own label
Sales	5 000	1 000	2 500	1 500
Cost of goods	2 500	500	1 325	975
Gross profit	2 500	500	1 175	525
Salesforce expense	125	125	219	131
Advertising/exhibition	80	16	40	24
Sales promotion	70	143	357	0
General admin.	990	198	494	293
Total expense	1 265	482	1 110	448
Net profit	1 235	180	650	770
Net profit %	24.7	1.8	2.6	5.1

expenditure have only minimal impact on retail branded goods sales, then the independent and chain DIY sectors will also cease to be profitable.

An analysis, therefore, which examines financial performance by 'business sector not consolidated' statements will often be more informative. This type of approach for Smith Ltd would (one hopes) lead the marketing department to undertake market research investigating the underlying causes of the poor financial performance in the retail sector before precipitately enacting price reductions or revised promotional spending.

According to Morden,[5] a management information system (MIS) is a 'formal system which enables organization members to access and transform stored data so as to provide information that will support the process of planning, organizing, directing and controlling the activities of the business'. Accounting transactions in any organization tend to be one of the most fully documented areas of activity. Hence it is frequently advocated that the marketing department would benefit from creating a management accounting system as a core element in their diagnostic control system.[6]

Despite the obvious benefits of adding management accounting capability to the control system, very few companies have progressed this concept beyond the point of analysing sales revenue by market sector.[4] Only a minority of organizations have extended the process to include measurement of costs for specific products, sales territories or distribution channels. In consequence, marketing departments are rarely able to operate a diagnostic control system that examines profit performance across different market sectors and/or product lines.[7]

In part this situation can be explained by the usual problems associated with allocating costs within an organization on anything other than a functional cost centre basis. Furthermore, the system designer has to grapple with a somewhat rare accounting principle; namely, that certain areas of marketing expenditure have a lagged—as opposed to an immediate—impact on revenue (e.g., advertising expenditure in the last quarter has minimal effect on sales until the next financial year).

The other contributory factor in the low adoption rate for the technique is that all managers tend to create information systems to justify existing personal opinions, not to enhance overall corporate understanding.[8] Marketeers are no exception to this rule and, as illustrated by the Smith case, cannot be expected to be advocates of a control mechanism that might contradict their current perceptions of opportunities to improve financial performance.

INTEGRATIVE CONTROL

The key input variable for other departments in many companies is the sales forecast. A production department will use these data to determine raw material procurement needs and production schedules, and to establish stock levels for finished goods. The accounting group will subsequently use the sales and production figures to calculate short-term and long-term borrowing requirements.

Once a plan is in progress, any revision in sales forecast will have a potentially dramatic impact on other departments, especially if the marketing group decides that the original sales forecast was too high. So it is critical that any control system has the capability to assess immediately the impact of a change in sales forecast on other groups within the organization.

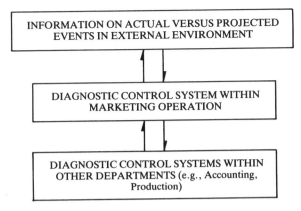

Figure 9.4 Integrative diagnostic control system.

In designing an effective diagnostic system, therefore, the marketing department should endeavour to include an integrative component that will fulfil this requirement (Fig. 9.4). The ultimate aim of such a system is to enable the marketing group to execute a series of alternative planning scenarios and determine the optimal action should a revision in sales forecast be deemed appropriate. This can usually only be achieved by building a computer model that combines the input/output relationships for both physical and financial resources in the form of a series of interactive equations. The implications of alternative scenarios can then be discussed with managers from other departments prior to a final decision being made on changes in the marketing mix.

At the point where the marketing MIS incorporates some form of modelling capability that permits the simulation of alternative propositions, the company's control mechanisms have then become a marketing decision support system (MDSS).[9] If only more marketeers recognized that MDSS is not a threat, but instead that it greatly extends their capability to analyse marketing mix performance, then surely their 'anti-control' attitude would finally disappear.

PROACTIVE CONTROL

The usual approach in marketing planning is to develop a three- to five-year long-range plan that provides a generalized outline of financial objectives and an overall statement of strategy. Detailed financial targets and accurate definitions of the marketing mix are then specified in the annual marketing plan.

The majority of the periodic and diagnostic systems described earlier compare actual performance with the annual plan. This means that any

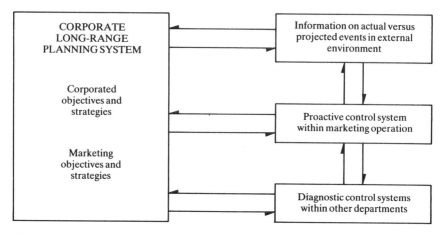

Figure 9.5 Proactive integrative diagnostic control system.

resultant revision in marketing objectives is related to historic targets that were established at the beginning of the financial year. In fact, history is a somewhat arbitrary model. Even more importantly it is the future, not the past, that is of concern to the organization. This perspective may possibly be rejected by a company operating in a very stable, completely unchanging business environment. However, as most organizations face increasingly volatile and uncertain market conditions, it is vital that proactive control systems are created which utilize the diagnosis of variance in current performance as the basis for examining the potential impact on the future long-term prospects of the organization.

A proactive control system can be created by linking the output from the integrative control system to the performance variables used in the long-range plan (Fig. 9.5). It is obviously not necessary to rewrite the long-range plan every time variance is identified in current performance. The data flow to the plan can be restricted to issues that are considered to have potential significant impact over the longer term.

Major impact issues will typically be those that represent either obstacles or opportunities such as a massive shift in market demand, technological breakthroughs, changes in strategy by competitors and significant variation in socio-political conditions. Where such events are identified, the marketing department can implement an assessment to determine whether the new circumstances can be managed within the current resource budget or if there is a need to radically alter the objectives and strategies specified in the long-range plan.

To illustrate a proactive system, it is assumed that a market research study by Wood Care Ltd revealed three factors most likely to limit market size in the future. These were (*a*) a trend towards house builders installing wood products that had been prestained at the supplier factory, (*b*) greater acceptance of plastic laminates for kitchen or bedroom furniture and (*c*) a rapidly growing preference for window and door frames to be made from maintenance-free uPVC or plastic–aluminium composites. This situation is not only going to influence current sales, but implies even greater problems in the future because total market size will at best remain static and may even go into decline. Therefore, in order to sustain corporate growth, the company may have to examine such actions as new product diversification, vertical integration or business acquisitions as alternatives to the current plan of attempting to expand sales for the existing line of wood stain products.

Although most marketeers now accept that 'the only predictable thing is change' in market environments, at the moment very few appear to place any great priority on incorporating a proactive link into existing control systems. This myopic attitude is possibly one of the key reasons why so many companies realize too late that performance will soon be constrained by technological change or rising competitive pressures. Unless marketeers are encouraged by senior managers to link together control and long-range planning systems, the only certain event in an increasingly volatile world is that more organizations will fail owing to an inadequate response to 'weak danger signals' initially generated in variance reports on current year performance.

A critical issue in the speed with which proactive MDSS will be adopted by the marketeer is the effectiveness of the user interface. The manager can only use a system if there is access to the right software, terminals, data files and an ability to build appropriate models. The enormity of fulfilling all these requirements has been highlighted by Little.[10] A recent major breakthrough occurred when software designers realized that the computer, not the manager, should be left to do the technically complex work of handling the data. As a result, software is now becoming available which is easily understood by the manager, who is no longer required to take in-depth courses in subjects such as FORTRAN programming before being able to operate the department's MDSS facilities.

REFERENCES

1. K. P. Fletcher, 'Computers for efficient utilization of resources', *Management Decisions*, vol. 21 (2), 1983.
2. J. M. Hulbert and N. E. Toy, 'A strategic framework for marketing control', *Journal of Marketing*, vol. 41, April 1977.
3. R. A. Feder, 'How to measure marketing performance', *Harvard Business Review*, May 1965.
4. L. S. Rayburn, 'Marketing costs: accountants to the rescue', *Management Accounting*, January 1981.
5. A. R. Morden, 'Management information systems; role and policy in an organizational context', *Management Decisions*, vol. 23 (2), 1985.

6. F. H. Mossman, I. M. Fischer and W. J. E. Crissy, *Financial Dimensions of Marketing Management*, Wiley, 1978.

7. R. M. S. Wilson and A. Bancroft, *The Application of Management Accounting Techniques to the Planning and Control of Marketing of Consumer Non-durables*, Institute of Cost and Management Accountants, July 1983.

8. M. S. Feldman and J. S. March, 'Information in organizations as signal and symbol', *Administrative Science Quarterly*, vol. 26, June 1981.

9. S. Alter, *Decision Support Systems: Current Practices and Continuing Challenges*, Addison-Wesley, 1980.

10. J. D. C. Little, 'Decision support systems for marketing managers', *Journal of Marketing*, vol. 43, (3), Summer 1979.

CHAPTER TEN

INTEGRATING THE MANUFACTURING AND MARKETING OPERATIONS

THE INTERRELATIONSHIPS BETWEEN MANUFACTURING AND MARKETING

Production executives in manufacturing industries are dependent upon sales forecasts from the marketing department if they are to match current output to customer orders and to plan the capacity required to fulfil new product development strategies in the future. One would expect, therefore, to find a close working relationship between the two departments, as illustrated in Fig. 10.1. Unfortunately, the main contact between the production staff and the marketeers usually occurs when the marketing group wish to complain about variance in the cost of finished goods, shortages of inventory on-hand versus orders pending, and product rejected by the customer; and further investigation of these situations often reveals that the marketing staff caused the problem in the first place. For example, the marketing group decides to increase price, gives customers prior notification of the change but neglects to warn the manufacturing department. Customer reaction to the announcement is to double the size of their orders whereupon insufficient finished goods are available to cover the short-term surge in sales. Had the marketing group informed the manufacturing department of their intentions, production schedules could have been revised and the inventory level increased to meet customer demand.

A possible reason for poor interdepartmental liaison is that, until recently, corporate policy in both North American and European companies gave 'favoured status' to the marketing and/or finance groups. Meanwhile production staff were usually treated as 'second class citizens' in terms of

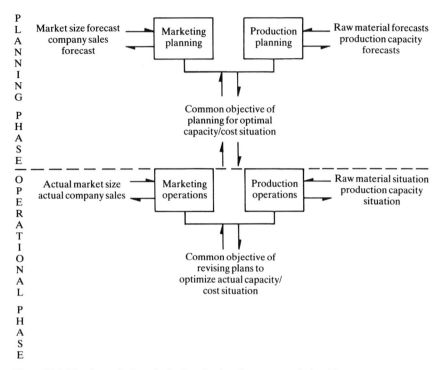

Figure 10.1 The theoretical marketing/production department relationship.

career prospects and salaries.[1, 2, 3] In the consumer goods sector, a further influence is the accepted corporate culture that production executives should serve the needs of the marketing group because the latter's activities have the greatest influence on the destiny of the organization.

Over the last few years there has been a realization that production executives can make a contribution to corporate performance at least equal to, and in some instances greater than, other functional groups within the organization.[3, 4] This change in perspective has in part been stimulated by the political realization that a country's survival is dependent upon the capability of manufacturing industries to stay ahead of competition in global markets. North America and Europe contain numerous examples of companies who ignored the advances in manufacturing expertise being achieved by Pacific Basin countries. At first, sales were lost in export markets. Then the new competitors from the Far East entered home markets of western nation companies and decimated the companies who failed to reinvest in modern, cost-effective production facilities (e.g., Taiwanese companies producing consumer electronic goods; the Korean shipbuilding industry; the Japanese office machine manufacturers).

Western companies who have successfully defended their markets

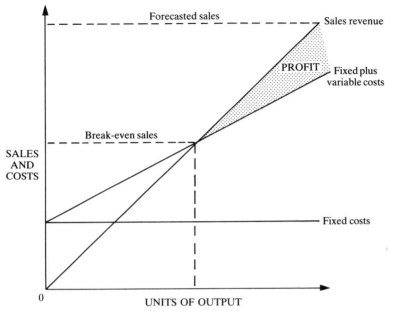

Figure 10.2*a* Forecasted performance.

against overseas competition are those who recognize the importance of the manufacturing function within the organization. In addition, such companies insist on close working relationships between their marketing and manufacturing operations.[5] This can only occur when the marketeers (*a*) have a clear understanding of the impact of production costs on profitability and (*b*) comprehend the synergistic benefits of working closely with production in areas such as capacity planning, product improvement programmes and new product development projects.

COST OF GOODS

Costs in a typical manufacturing operation can be classified into fixed and variable. The latter include items such as raw materials and labour, which rise and fall in direct relation to output. Interaction between these two forms of cost, sales revenue and profit can be illustrated by a graph of the type shown in Fig. 10.2*a*. Break-even is the point on the plot where revenue from sales is equal to total cost. Beyond this point, revenue exceeds costs and the company moves into a positive profit situation.

The break-even chart can be used to demonstrate why certain actions by the marketing department can have an adverse impact on profit. One possible situation (Fig. 10.2*b*) is where actual sales are less than budget and profit is

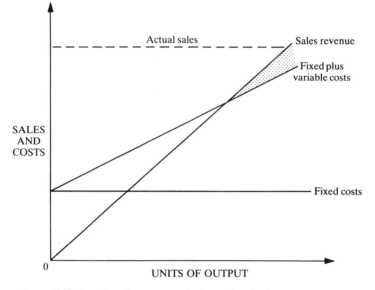

Figure 10.2*b* Actual performance—sales lower than budget.

reduced. Alternatively, the marketing group may consider that market conditions demand a price decrease. Although the company still achieves the forecasted unit sales volume, the lower price results in profit again being below budget (Fig. 10.2*c*). A third possibility is that although the forecasted sales revenue is achieved, there are significant unexpected fluctuations in sales by month across the financial year. In order to handle the extreme volatility in the pattern of orders, the production group are forced to resort to overtime and temporary second shifts during periods of higher than expected demand. This action causes a major increase in costs and although sales are as forecasted, profit will be reduced (Fig. 10.2*d*).

OVERHEAD ABSORPTION

Costs such as equipment maintenance, plant refurbishments, supervisory and administrative staff salaries are incurred even when a plant operation is inactive. Many companies operate some form of standard cost system through which fixed costs are usually recovered by allocating them as overhead costs to each unit of production. If output does not reach forecasted levels, then some of this burden remains unabsorbed. When approaching year end and the marketing group faces a shortfall in sales versus forecast, one popular solution is to announce a massive sales promotion. Intermediaries will bring forward their future orders so as to take

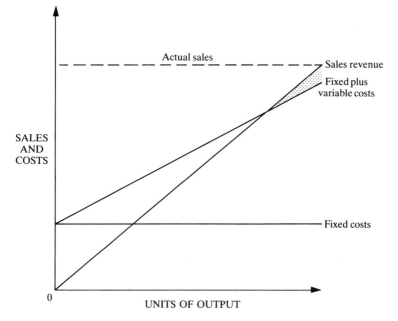

Figure 10.2*c* Actual performance—sales at lower than budgeted unit price.

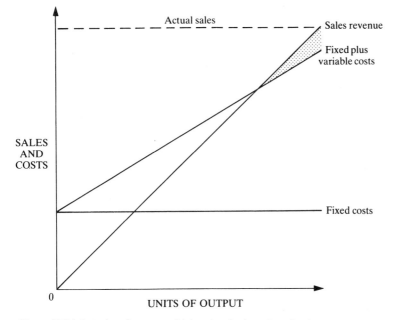

Figure 10.2*d* Actual performance—higher than budgeted production costs.

Table 10.1 Example of impact of first quarter unallocated burden being absorbed later in year

	Budgeted performance (£'000)		Actual performance (£'000)	
	Quarter 1	Total year	Quarter 1	Total year
Sales	1000	5000	500	4500
Cost of goods	600	3000	300	2820
(% of sales)	(60)	(60)	(60)	(62.7)
Overhead burden cost component	240	1200	120	1200
(% of sales)	(24)	(24)	(24)	(26.7)
Gross profit	400	2000	200	1680
(% of sales)	(40)	(40)	(40)	(37.3)

advantage of the short-term promotional discounts. They will then hold stock in excess of actual needs and it may be some months before they re-order any product. The production department will face a period in the early months of the next financial year when sales are almost zero. In the first quarter of the new financial year, costs will be allocated as per budget and the marketing group will assume that cost of goods will remain as forecasted. However, unless there is a major surge in sales later in the year, overhead costs, which were assumed to be absorbed in the first quarter, will remain unallocated because there has been insufficient production. Eventually an adjustment will have to be made to cost of goods to add back the unallocated burden, resulting in a significant reduction in gross profit. This effect is demonstrated in Table 10.1, for an example company where sales were 50 per cent below budget in the first quarter and recovered in subsequent months. Allocation of unabsorbed burden to sales later in the year reduced the gross profit margin from the forecasted 40 per cent of sales to an actual of 37.3 per cent.

ECONOMIC ORDER QUANTITY

Production managers spend their life balancing the two variables of production efficiency and the cost of holding stocks of finished goods. Long production runs of an item will minimize manufacturing costs because operatives are at their most productive. Also, no time is lost in stopping lines while equipment is changed for the manufacture of a different product. Long production runs in excess of current demand will, however, create large stocks of finished goods which cost money to store and incur interest charges if external borrowing is necessary to fund the increase in current assets. Optimizing the balance between length of production run and inventory costs is usually managed by establishing an economic order quantity (EOQ) for each product. Once the level of finished goods in the inventory falls below a predefined level, the quantity specified by the EOQ is scheduled for production.

The EOQ process is effective as long as sales patterns are stable or the sales trend is upwards. However, once a product enters the decline phase of the PLC, sustaining an appropriate EOQ can become a nightmare. If a production run is set at a level that ensures optimum production efficiency, the high level of output will mean that finished goods remain in inventory for many months. The alternative—manufacturing only a small quantity of the product—will resolve the inventory cost problem but be accompanied by a rise in production costs. A company will therefore benefit from their marketing department's appreciation of this problem and their willingness to discontinue items that have entered the decline phase.

Where a slow-moving product is regarded as important to a key customer, an alternative to discontinuation is to classify the product as a 'produce-to-order item'. Customers are informed of this change in product status and also of the minimum order size required before the goods can be scheduled for manufacture. In this way, the item is only produced after an adequate-sized order has been received. The customer must also be willing to accept a delay before the goods can be delivered as they are not held in inventory. The marketing department may argue that to impose these conditions on the product will damage customer relations and may request that the product remains within the EOQ system. If the production department accede to this request they may well be criticized by the accounting department for creating excess inventory levels that will lead to higher interest charges and reduce ROI. These criticisms will probably be followed by a further worsening of the working relationship between marketeers and production staff. Such problems can be avoided if the company adopts a 'system selling' or 'programmed merchandising' management philosophy which involves a regular analysis of product performance at the customer level. The salesforce can demonstrate to their customers how they can improve profitability by ceasing to stock the company's slow-moving goods. Acceptance of the recommendation then allows the company to avoid 'produce-to-order' goods in the product range.

JUST IN TIME

As lot size increases, production set-up costs fall but inventory costs rise. The sum of these two costs represents a trade-off between each other and total costs will be at a minimum if set-up and inventory costs are equal. It is this point that determines the EOQ for a product. Should it prove feasible to further reduce set-up costs then this will permit a lowering of the EOQ level.

The Japanese have long recognized that if emphasis is placed on reducing set-up costs, then lot size and inventory costs will also fall. Western managers have tended to favour the approach of having 'buffer stocks' in order to insulate the manufacturing department from unexpected surges in demand. With the Japanese approach, however, inventory levels will become smaller and the buffering effect of holding excess finished goods is removed. This philosophy of small lot sizes and minimal finished goods holdings has become known as 'just in time' or 'JIT' manufacturing.[6]

The marketeer can play a very important role in optimizing the productivity gains that can be provided by JIT. One contribution is to persuade customers, through the salesforce, to cease placing last-minute large orders and demanding instant delivery. Additional smoothing of production schedules may also be achieved by reducing the frequency of sales promotion events during the year. The most vital role, however, is to develop closer links with the customer in order to convince them of the benefits of sharing information that will increase the accuracy of the demand forecasts used in preparing JIT production schedules. This change in the company/customer relationship can only occur if the customer is convinced that there are mutual benefits in a more disciplined approach to ordering, fewer sales promotions and a pooling of knowledge. Hence, the marketing department may have to implement a programme of customer education on the concept of JIT and also be prepared to share the benefits of enhanced productivity through price reduction or quality enhancement. If the marketeer merely perceives JIT as a mechanism to increase corporate profitability, this can only place a strain on customer relations, which will result in lost sales over the longer term.

TOTAL QUALITY MANAGEMENT

Another aspect of Japanese manufacturing philosophy is to emphasize the importance of quality throughout the entire production cycle and thereby reduce the number of rejected goods returned by the customer for replacement or repair. Originally developed by Americans,[7, 8] the concept is known as total quality management (TQM). This involves training all employees to be more quality orientated and to actively seek mechanisms to further enhance quality through changes in manufacturing processes. The marketing department can make a significant contribution to quality management by understanding how their requirements for product performance can create quality problems for the manufacturing department. Where the manufacturing team identifies difficulties in meeting a product specification, the marketing department should be willing to undertake market research to determine whether a revision to the product specification is acceptable to the customer. For example, a processor is having problems with the flesh: batter ratio of 45:55 + 1.0 per cent for a frozen, battered chicken product. The marketing department therefore undertakes a ship test to determine whether a move to 45:55 + 3.0 per cent flesh: batter ratio is as acceptable to national chain account customers in the catering sector.

In many industrial markets, a company will manufacture a product based upon a specification drawn up by the customer. The specification may create problems for the company because the customer does not have an in-depth understanding of the limitations of the production processes involved. There are usually major benefits, therefore, in including representatives from the manufacturing group in the project team negotiating the contract with the customer. They will be able to identify immediately any specifications that would increase costs (e.g., the size tolerance for a component; the maximum voltage load that a circuit must be capable of handling). Discussion can then take place to revise the proposed specification and, possibly, lead to a faster delivery or a reduction in the contract price.

PRODUCT IMPROVEMENT PROGRAMMES

A standard approach for extending the life of a product in the late maturity/early decline phase of the PLC is to introduce a new, improved product. The usual method is for the marketing department to identify, by market research or their own judgement, the desired area of performance enhancement. The R&D/production personnel are then requested to develop a formulation or produce a specification capable of delivering the desired change.

This very simplistic, one-way communication process represents a failure to exploit fully the expertise contained within the manufacturing group. A potentially more beneficial approach would be to provide the manufacturing group with a complete briefing on the desired requirements on cost or performance parameters and the relationship between these variables and market conditions. One way of doing this is to use a product performance/market price policy matrix of the type illustrated in Fig. 10.3.

At any point in time, the marketing group may be seeking assistance to improve perhaps one or two areas of the product line (e.g., the company is concerned about the product in cell 8 of the policy matrix and is seeking a product upgrade to provide the basis of a price increase). By being provided with a complete review of product line strategy, the R&D/production personnel (a) will be in a much better position to comment on the technical feasibility of the marketing group's requests and (b) may be stimulated to propose an alternative strategy of greater long-term benefit to the organization.

REQUIRED FUTURE PRODUCT PERFORMANCE

	Reduce	Same	Improve	
	(1)	(2)	(3)	
Decrease	Product performance incompatible with market – need for major de-engineering and price reduction programme	Reasonably competitive market requiring a reduced cost product formulation to permit price reduction	Highly competitive market environment demanding significant product modernization and cost reduction to sustain future sales	
	(4)	(5)	(6)	
Same	Reasonably competitive market but opportunity to enhance profit margin by lowering product performance	Current situation monitor opportunity for future enhancement	Reasonably competitive market requiring product performance upgrade that can be delivered without need for price increase	PROPOSED FUTURE PRICING STRATEGY
	(7)	(8)	(9)	
Increase	Company in very dominant market position but customer attitudes indicate profit improvement opportunity from de-engineering and price increase	Reasonably competitive market but opportunity to increase price. To justify move, market should be provided with an upgraded product	Increasingly competitive market but opportunity to avoid price competition through significant upgrade in performance for which customer willing to accept higher price	

Figure 10.3 Performance/price product planning matrix.

PRODUCT DEVELOPMENT PROGRAMMES

Studies of military aircraft production during the Second World War showed that, as output increased, unit production costs declined. This effect has become known as the 'experience curve'. It is usually illustrated as a graph of log production costs against log output, because this generates a linear plot. As the experience curve concept has a number of important implications for new product development, it is therefore vital that marketing staff work in close cooperation with the manufacturing group in order to fully understand the issues involved.[9]

Firstly, a market leader, having typically sold more product, will have a cost of production advantage over competition. Hence in a scenario of the type illustrated in Fig. 10.4, company B would be ill-advised to consider launching a similar product and mounting a head-to-head confrontation with company A. For the latter can choose to react either by cutting price or by using the larger gap between current price and costs to fund a massive promotional counter-attack. In these circumstances, the marketing staff of

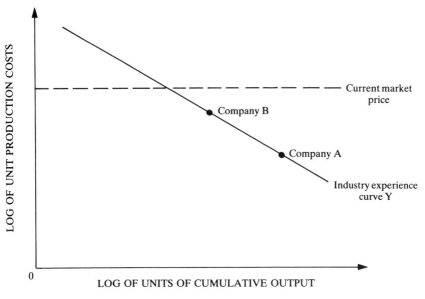

Figure 10.4 Relationship between costs and market price.

company B should review with the manufacturing group whether any opportunity exists to use a new technology as the basis for creating a new experience curve that would overcome the current cost advantage enjoyed by company A (Fig. 10.5).

The slope of the experience curve will also influence decisions about the desired speed for market expansion of new product introductions and the

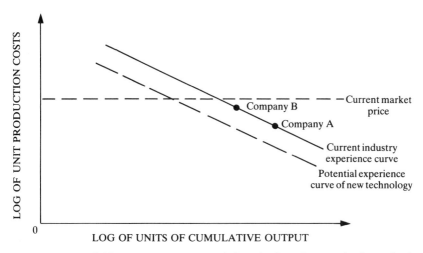

Figure 10.5 Potential for company to compete via introduction of new production technology.

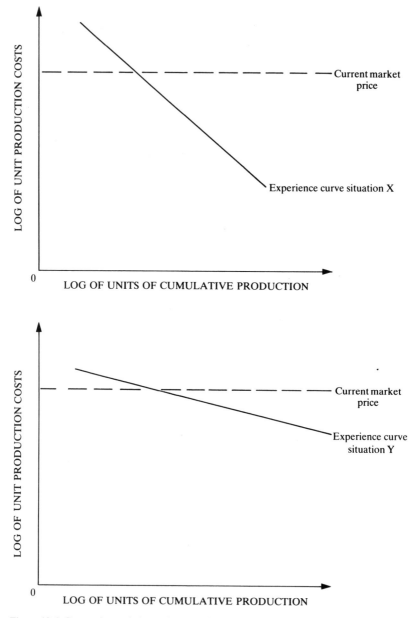

Figure 10.6 Comparison of alternative experience curve scenarios.

strategic advantages of horizontal or vertical integration strategies. In the scenario shown in Fig. 10.6, the company is early into new technologies that have different experience curves. Situation X offers the opportunity for major cost reduction benefits from expansion of output. Thus a strategy to expand market size or share rapidly, through aggressive promotion or price reduction, should be considered. This will then permit the company to establish a secure market position based upon manufacturing efficiency prior to competitors being attracted to the market. In contrast, situation Y offers minimal cost savings because the slope of the experience curve is much flatter. In these circumstances speed of market expansion is less critical, and the marketing department would probably select a product strategy based upon performance differentiation or niche positioning as the path to protecting the company from price-based competitive pressures in the future.

There is frequently a significant difference in the slope of the experience curve at different levels in the same industry. A hypothetical example of this effect is illustrated in Fig. 10.7 for a multinational wholesaler in the shrimp industry. Should the company forecast increased competition at the wholesale level, they may decide that there would be little economy of scale advantage in opening new wholesale outlets. Instead, they may decide that there is much greater benefit in acquiring one or more manufacturing operations and thereby exploit the experience curve benefits that are available if one can dominate this level of the shrimp industry. In contrast, unless raw material shortages are expected to develop, there is little advantage in moving into the catching or peeling sectors of the industry because the experience curves are relatively flat.

The failure of marketeers to work jointly with manufacturing personnel in developing a better understanding of how the effects of an experience curve provide opportunities to strengthen marketing strategies has been a major influence in the decline of many companies in both Europe and North America. In order to avoid a repetition of this in the future, marketing department plans should be required to include an analysis of the experience curve in relation to potential impact on both current and new product development strategies.[10]

CAPACITY PLANNING

The marketing department's analysis of experience curve effects can also be invaluable to the manufacturing group because it can identify the areas of the production operation that should receive priority for the allocation of investment funds and R&D resources when planning capacity expansion schemes. Where analysis reveals that the company is incapable of exploiting an experience curve situation, then marketing and manufacturing executives can work together to determine whether the company can protect itself from

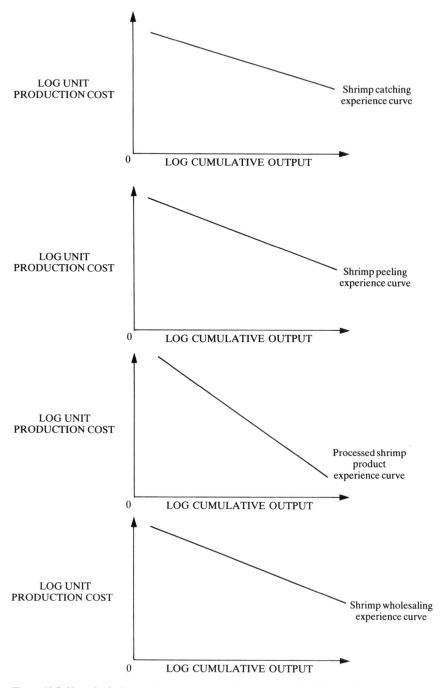

Figure 10.7 Hypothetical experience curves at various levels in the shrimp industry.

price-based competition by establishing a product development programme to strengthen the company's quality/product performance superiority suited to a specific customer segment in the market.[11]

Experience curve assessments will also be of assistance to the manufacturing group when it is considering subcontracting or plant relocation. If the marketing department has clearly articulated its decision to sustain a long-term market position based on a cost advantage over competition, then concentration of manufacturing facilities on large-scale sites and minimizing the level of subcontracting may be a preferred production strategy. Alternatively, if the marketing strategy is that of specialist product positioning, this might be best supported by a production strategy involving smaller satellite plants located near to key customers and the development of close working relationships with subcontractors to optimize the balance between fixed and variable costs at these satellite facilities.

Capacity planning is one of the most critical strategic decisions facing a firm because project implementation usually entails irreversible large-scale expenditure on fixed assets. In all cases the marketing department will be required to provide forecasts of total industry demand and probable behaviour of competitors.

Companies seek to add capacity in order to sustain or improve market share. Underestimation of market demand is rarely a major problem if the organization is able to add capacity at a later date. The more dangerous position is where the marketing department are excessively optimistic and the company is left with capacity greatly in excess of achievable sales.

The risks of excess capacity are greatly exacerbated in those industries that exhibit the following characteristics:[12, 13]

- The most effective exploitation of production technology involves a step-shaped capacity expansion curve.
- Products are not differentiated, buyer choice is heavily influenced by price, and customer loyalty is based purely on a company's ability to fulfil orders placed.
- Demand is cyclical and/or significantly influenced by the overall prevailing economic conditions.
- There is a long lead time between the decision to add capacity and the company's ability to bring the new plant on-stream.

These features are common in the petrochemical, mining, steel, fertilizer and paper-manufacturing industries. For a company seeking to attain a dominant market share in these types of industry, the ultimate objective is to have a final scale of operations that closely matches forecasted sales at market maturity. However, in order not to lose sales to competitors during the market growth phase, it will usually be necessary to operate with capacity in excess of current demand (Fig. 10.8a). As the decision points for new plant investment all occur very early in the PLC, it is imperative that the marketing

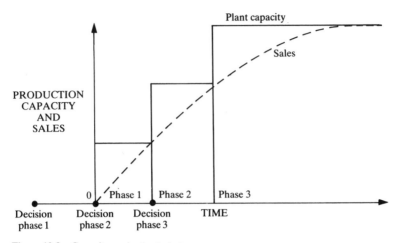

Figure 10.8*a* Capacity and sales in balance.

and production planning staff work very closely together to monitor and assess the implications of any variation of sales patterns from forecast.

Figure 10.8*b* shows that if the company proceeded with the original capacity plan, then at market maturity the company will be unable to fully meet customer demand. However a probably more disastrous scenario is that illustrated in Fig. 10.8*c* where early sales indicate that market demand at maturity will leave the company with a massive level of excess capacity. This may be the result of an overestimate of total industry size and/or a much more intensive competitive climate than was assumed in earlier predictions of

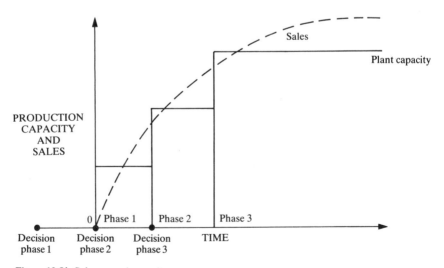

Figure 10.8*b* Sales exceed capacity.

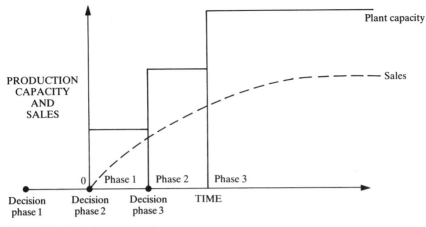

Figure 10.8c Capacity exceeds sales.

future market conditions. At the point when the excess capacity situation is recognized by the planners, the company will be forced to terminate plant construction even though there is little hope of recovering the sizeable funds already invested in the phase 3 operation. In the most extreme situation, the company may have no need for a significant proportion of existing capacity and be forced to 'mothball' manufacturing capacity in the hope that market demand will improve in the future. The alternative is to embark on a massive programme of price discounting in an attempt to stimulate demand and/or drive competitors out of the market. Whichever path is selected, the company faces an extensive period of minimal or no profits—a situation that might have been avoided had the marketing group originally forecasted future performance more accurately.

REFERENCES

1. 'A drastic new loss of competitive strength', *Business Week*, 30 June 1980.
2. R. H. Hayes and W. J. Abernathy, 'Managing our way to economic decline', *Harvard Business Review*, July 1980.
3. W. J. Abernathy, K. B. Clark and A. M. Hanchow, *Industrial Renaissance Producing a Competitive Future for America*, Basic Books, 1983.
4. P. R. Witt, *Cost Effective Products*, Reston Publishing, 1986.
5. R. T. Pascale and A. G. Athos, *The Art of Japanese Management*, Penguin, 1982.
6. R. J. Schonberger, *Japanese Manufacturing Techniques: Nine Hidden Lessons in Simplicity*, Free Press, 1982.
7. A. Feigenbaum, *Total Quality Control: Engineering and Management*, McGraw-Hill, 1961.
8. P. B. Crosby, *Quality Is Free: the Art of Making Quality Certain*, McGraw-Hill, 1979.
9. K. Ohmae, *The Mind of the Strategist*, Penguin, 1983.
10. A. C. Cooper and D. Schendel, 'Strategic responses to technological threats', *Business Horizons*, February 1976.

11. F. W. Gluck and R. N. Foster, 'Managing technological change: a box of cigars for Brad', *Harvard Business Review*, September 1975.
12. M. E. Porter, *Competitive Strategy: Techniques for Analysing Industry and Competitors*, Free Press, 1980.
13. W. E. Fruhan Jr, *The Fight for Competitive Advantage*, Division of Research, Harvard Graduate School of Business Administration, 1972.

ELEVEN

THE 'Ps' AND 'Q' OF SERVICE MARKETING

SERVICE MARKETING

A characteristic of the economies of western nations is the increasing importance of service industries as a proportion of gross national product (GNP) and as a source of employment. Various factors have influenced the growth of the service industry sector. In consumer markets, many people can now afford to purchase a much broader range of goods, including leisure products such as holidays, participate in expensive sports, and delegate many household functions such as repairs or decorating to external providers. These same consumers, along with individuals within industrial organizations, are increasingly purchasing technologically complex products. New firms have evolved to sustain operation of these advanced technology systems by providing maintenance and training services.

As a country gains economic wealth, it can afford to fund a major expansion of public sector organizations that are also engaged in the provision of services such as education, housing and health care. Although these may be made available on a non-profit basis, it is nevertheless recognized that effective management of public sector services will involve application of appropriate management philosophies. The same concepts are increasingly being applied by non-profit private sector organizations such as charities and religious institutions.

Marketeers have not been slow in identifying new opportunities for their own services. Over recent years, a wealth of publications have debated the issue of whether the marketing management task in the service sector differs from that found in tangible goods markets. Undoubtedly the debate will continue well into the future, but it does seem that the service markets exhibit certain important characteristics[1] which include intangibility, inseparability, heterogeneity, perishability and ownership.

Intangibility

The product may be partially or totally intangible. A meal in a restaurant, for instance, contains elements of tangibility (e.g., the food) and intangibility (e.g., the service provided by the staff). In contrast, a life assurance policy can be considered as purely intangible goods. Lovelock[2] has proposed that 'a good is an object, a device, a thing: a service is a deed, a performance, an effort'. Ultimately, however, most services offered to a market combine tangible and intangible elements. The factor that governs a product being considered as goods or a service is the customer's perception of whether the purchase is an intangible or a tangible item.

Inseparability

In most cases the production and consumption of a service are inseparable because there is a simultaneous production and consumption of the product (e.g., a stockbroker providing advice to a client on an appropriate selection of stocks in which to invest).

Heterogeneity

As people are usually involved, the delivery of a service product exhibits heterogeneity because it is difficult to standardize the output when a large number of employees are engaged in its provision (e.g., customers being served by different staff in a large store). In addition, customers often have heterogeneous needs for the type of service required.

Perishability

Services are a perishable product and they usually cannot be stored. Thus an inability to provide the service because of capacity constraint will mean the sale is lost for ever (e.g., a fully booked hotel has no bedrooms available to prospective additional customers).

Ownership

The supplier of a service will usually retain ownership and the customer will have use of a facility for a limited period (e.g., a customer hiring a vehicle from a truck rental company).

THE CONTRIBUTION OF MARKETEERS TO SERVICE INDUSTRIES—THE NEW 'Ps'

Marketeers have correctly identified that many organizations, by being product rather than customer orientated, were offering services based on the organization's perceptions of market needs (e.g., product offerings in the consumer sector of the UK insurance industry).[3] Marketeers hired either as employees or advisers by such organizations rapidly justified the use of market research to provide a better understanding of customer requirements. Data from such studies also showed that market demand is not homogeneous and this, in turn, raised doubts over the practice of supplying the same products across all groups of potential customers.

Adoption of a marketing-orientated operating philosophy in a service sector is usually followed by the launch of new products designed to meet more effectively the varying customer needs in the market. This phenomenon is illustrated by the rapid growth in the number of companies offering credit cards in the UK. Given that the size of the population limits total market size, the card companies are now positioning their products to appeal to specific user segments (e.g., the lower interest Chase Visa card offered only to good credit risk customers).[4]

Marketeers who moved from tangible goods operations into the service sector soon found that the factors of intangibility, inseparability and heterogeneity presented major obstacles for any organization wishing to stabilize or expand customer demand. Furthermore, management of the marketing process was often made more difficult because market research revealed that customers perceived all companies within any service sector to be offering the same products (e.g., solicitors advising companies on employment legislation or health and safety laws). In attempting to manage these issues, marketeers identified the importance of the new 'Ps' of People, Physical evidence and Process as vital elements used by customers in their evaluation of the quality of services received.

Company personnel, especially those in direct contact with the customer, can rarely be separated from the service being provided (e.g., a programmer installing an MRP system for a manufacturing company). Hence, a key factor in the customer's judgement of product quality will be the appearance and behaviour of the employee representing the supplier.

The importance of the customer/employee interaction has been demonstrated by comparative research of the US airline, hotel and restaurant industries.[5] If problems are to occur between customers and staff it will usually be caused by a failure in communication. The obvious scenario is that of misunderstanding (e.g., the sales manager who stressed the importance of conference facilities at time of booking a hotel, only to arrive and find no meeting rooms are available). A more complex situation is where a failure to communicate has created customer expectations that are greater than the supplier is able to provide.

Following the deregulation of the US airline industry, fares declined and people were encouraged to make more flights and travel to more distant locations. Airline promotions had previously focused on the enjoyable, exciting prospect of aeroplane travel. What passengers actually encountered were crowded terminals and flights, and airline personnel who were unable to provide the level of personal attention expected. As the airline industry could not afford to alter the people component by adding staff, a common solution was to reposition the product image through emphasizing the promotional concept of 'no frills service, but we will get you where you want to go'.

In addition to personnel, customers will use the physical features associated with the service provider as another indicator of product quality. To achieve a successful impression, the supplier will have to determine the expectations of the customer and then develop an appropriate overall corporate design covering physical facilities, appearance of employees and supporting collateral items (e.g., letterhead, brochures and display materials). A recent example of this total identity approach is that adopted by British Airways who, in seeking to present a superior quality/caring image, invested in a new corporate logo, redesigned ground and flight staff uniforms and refurbished their aircraft fleet both internally and externally.[6]

The other factor used by customers to judge product quality is the process associated with the smooth and efficient delivery of the service being purchased. A company seeking a listing on the USM would probably hire the services of a merchant bank to manage the share application and issue process. If, during the early phase of the relationship, the merchant bank produced a prospectus containing an incorrect financial statement, this would severely damage their credibility with the client company.

ACCEPTANCE OF MARKETEERS IN SERVICE ORGANIZATIONS

Although marketeers have made significant contributions towards improving the performance of service organizations, research as recent as 1984 in the UK showed that the marketing concept is still treated with suspicion by senior management.[7] Research of service companies has shown, for example, that many organizations still limit the marketing task to that of a staff role without granting the marketeer any authority over departments that directly interface with the customers. Furthermore, even where the marketing group is seen as an important entity within the organization, expenditure on market research is sometimes restricted because senior executives still insist on relying upon their own judgement to determine which services should be made available to the market.

In part, the slow acceptance of marketeers in service organizations reflects the cultural attitude that marketing is synonymous with selling and is therefore not really appropriate within a professional organization. This perspective remains common among institutions within the financial services and health care industries. However, in some organizations, another reason for the rejection of marketeers is an experience of having approved massive expenditure on new promotional campaigns only to find that this investment was not justified by the almost imperceptible increase in revenue. Where this viewpoint prevails, it can only be explained by the fact that marketeers involved lacked the managerial skills to fulfil their assigned responsibilities.

An example of errors in methodology was demonstrated by marketeers in the US retail financial services industry during early attempts in the seventies to expand the sales of banking services. Similar approaches have been adopted in the early eighties in the UK. In both cases, the first phase of marketing effort involved the use of major television advertising campaigns accompanied by expenditure on sales promotion such as self-liquidating premiums to stimulate customer trial. The measurement of success for the campaigns was the absolute number of new accounts opened. Although some new customers were attracted from the non-user segment, the majority of the new business came from individuals either switching from another bank or moving from single to multi-account banking. In certain cases, the consumers who switched loyalties because of dissatisfaction with their current bank were already known as 'problem customers'. These people were already unpopular because of their inability to manage their financial affairs, and their original bank was pleased to lose them to competition.

What must be of concern, however, are research findings which indicate that, despite significant promotional expenditure on communicating a more 'caring' attitude, many customers still hold a low opinion of the services they actually receive from their bank.[8, 9] One probable reason for the failure of the new promotional campaigns is that the banks' marketeers used classic fast-moving consumer goods (FMCG) marketing techniques that they had previously applied in building brand share for mass market tangible goods. As demonstrated in Table 11.1, however, there are significant differences between these two types of market.

Given these differences, it can be argued that the retail financial services sector should have placed greater emphasis on promotional systems linked to activities at point of purchase. Where an organization has control of the customer contact point, it is possible to employ personal selling techniques that can have an important impact on potential purchase behaviour. In these circumstances, reliance on purely mass market advertising techniques is possibly not the most appropriate way to utilize promotional funds.

Table 11.1 A comparison of the FMCG environment and the financial services sector

FMCG sector	Financial services
Customer requires minimal education prior to product adoption	Customer usually requires education prior to new product adoption
Customer needs are relatively homogeneous	Customer needs are highly heterogeneous, ranging from a simple current account through to complex investment services
Product is typically purchased in limited or self-service environment	Product purchase is in a high service level environment
Purchase frequency is high, brand loyalty variable, hence sales promotions have significant influence on sales volume	Product purchase frequency is relatively low, loyalty quite high, hence sales promotions have limited impact
Link to customer is through intermediaries who can influence marketing mix of suppliers	No intermediaries involved, hence no outside influence over marketing mix

THE CUSTOMER CARE CONCEPT FOR DELIVERING QUALITY IN SERVICE MARKETS

Given the difference between FMCG markets and the retail banking environment, in the second cycle of marketing effort many banks moved to (a) offering products specifically designed to fulfil needs in different customer segments and (b) placing greater emphasis on building customer loyalty at point of purchase. The key advantage in this approach is that a bank employee can use dialogue to identify the specific needs of various customer groups and respond by offering the most appropriate range of banking services.

Those organizations in the service sector who embrace a marketing-orientated managerial philosophy soon recognized that a vital element in creating a positive image is the effective control of the employee/customer interface. This usually occurs after the evaluation of early promotion-orientated marketing programmes indicates that they have not generated the expected major increase in revenue or market share. Furthermore, service organizations who operate in relatively homogeneous product sectors (e.g., estate agents and insurance brokers) have realized that the quality of service rendered by employees during contacts with customers can provide a vital weapon in the war to differentiate the organization from competition.[10]

Service organizations who identified the importance of the employee/customer interface, directed resources towards enhancing employee performance through training. Part of this training widened the employee's knowledge of company products and another part focused on improving their interpersonal skills. An immediate advantage of this investment in training is to reduce the variability of service provision by employees. In addition, as employees become more aware of the importance of their role, they will be prompted to propose to management any change in operations that could further enhance service levels (e.g., employees in a supermarket, recognizing the imbalance of staffing levels at checkouts, work with management to revise shifts and job roles to reduce queues during busy periods in the store). Such programmes should not be restricted to employees in direct contact with customers, but should extend throughout the organization by establishing a management culture that values a high quality of service in all job roles. In this way, other departments begin to contribute ideas to support quality (e.g., a credit control department who act to reduce the number of errors in customer invoices, which has been a source of complaint by both customers and company sales representatives).

This concept of enhancing quality has been encapsulated in an organizational operating philosophy known as 'customer care'.[11] It is now a fundamental aspect of managerial culture within many service industries (e.g., airlines, retail shops, hotels, fast food chains and utility companies).

MARKETEERS AND CUSTOMER CARE

Some marketeers are of the opinion that the main requirement for an effective customer care programme is to train staff who interact with the customer to be 'better at their job', and the marketeers will restrict their responsibilities to such activities as developing new advertising and sales promotion campaigns. In so doing, the marketing groups (a) will have missed an important opportunity to contribute towards improving the performance of their organization and (b) by handing the responsibility for quality management to the training or personnel department, will have weakened their perceived role in the management of the quality of service control processes.[12]

It should be recognized that there are three variables (Fig. 11.1) that influence the customer care process:

1. The product knowledge and interpersonal skills of the employees who interact with the customers.
2. The type of service required by the customers and their perception of how the organization fulfils their expectations on quality.
3. The organizational structure of the company, which determines the efficiency with which services are delivered at all phases from the point of initial contact through to the customer's post-purchase evaluation of the service received.

The installation of an effective customer care programme requires a three-phase process.[13] The first step is to define the nature and components

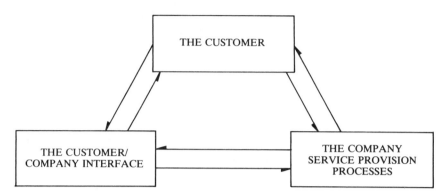

Figure 11.1 The customer care triangle.

that constitute the portfolio of services available to the prospective customers (e.g., a computer software consultancy group can supply a range of services from updating an existing program through to implementing a complete restructuring of a client's data management system). Each of the provided services can then be analysed to determine (*a*) the network of elements involved in the provision of the service, (*b*) the internal organizational processes that contribute to each element and (*c*) the contact points encountered by the customer during purchase and consumption of the service.

This detailed analysis will provide the basis for the second stage: defining the criteria through which customers will measure the quality of service received. Some of these criteria will involve tangible aspects of the service package (e.g., the cost and price for components used in updating a client's computer system). Other criteria will be based on tangible issues, such as the friendliness of staff and length of time taken to respond to a customer's complaint. For each of these criteria, a minimum standard will have to be established against which actual performance can then be measured.

It should be recognized that these standards must be based on fulfilling the expectations of the customer and must not merely reflect the judgement of the organization on what is acceptable to the market (e.g., the average time customers can expect to wait before a technician will arrive to repair a machine fault). Some standards can be based on existing company records (e.g., the cost of staff assigned to a specific project) and others will require market research in order to establish the requirements of potential customers.

Once these standards have been set, the third phase of the customer care programme is to organize regular sampling to determine whether there is any variance between actual and desired performance. As in the initial determination of standards, some information will be available from internal company records and other data will have to be obtained from surveys of customer attitudes. Where variance between desired and actual quality of service is identified, the organization must consider appropriate remedial action.

REMEDYING QUALITY PROBLEMS

Remedying an identified variance in the quality of service provision will usually involve a careful assessment of the cause of the problem. In some cases it may be caused by the poor performance of staff at the client interface (e.g., an employee who does not understand a computerized order entry system and makes mistakes in entering customer requirements). This type of problem can normally be rectified through further investment in staff training.

It may be the case, however, that the variance in quality is the result of inappropriate internal organizational processes. For example, an insurance company may require regional offices to forward to head office for approval any application for product liability coverage in excess of £1m. Owing to inadequate staffing levels, the application processing at head office is causing delays of up to twelve weeks between original application and final acceptance of the proposal. In the meantime, prospective clients become tired of waiting and file another application with a competitor who can usually provide coverage within four weeks. In order to improve the quality of service, the example company can either revise their procedures (e.g., delegate authority to the regional offices) or improve the workflow process at head office.

Analysis of quality problems may reveal a variance between the company's quality standard and that desired by the customer. A very common reason for this variance is that the customer has a greater expectation of quality than the organization is actually capable of delivering at a cost affordable by the client.

This problem is faced by the accounting profession in the UK, especially among their clients from the small business sector. Research[14] indicates a low level of satisfaction with the service received. The majority of clients do not realize that by improving their internal bookkeeping and management accounting systems, the resultant saving in audit fees could be utilized to purchase more in-depth financial advisory support services from their accountant.

To reach this point, however, clients will need assistance to upgrade their own accountancy skills. The more perceptive accountancy practices are now assisting their clients by providing or recommending training and/or supplying self-learning materials. The return on this investment is (a) improved client satisfaction over the quality of service provision and (b) an increase in new business generated by active 'word of mouth' recommendation by the satisfied existing client base.

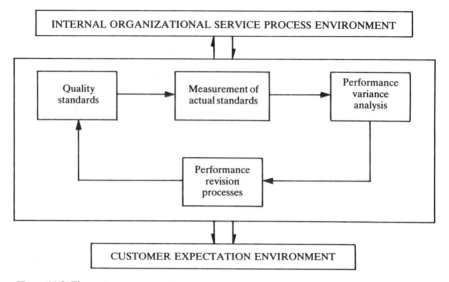

Figure 11.2 The customer care system.

FURTHER DEVELOPMENT OF THE CUSTOMER CARE SYSTEM

A marketing department is in the unique position of being able to link the market and the organization, thereby having the potential to further enhance a company's customer care system. It is therefore beneficial for marketeers to assess how the system can be more effective in areas such as defining the product service portfolio, setting quality standards, evaluating performance, diagnosing causes for quality variance, revising organizational processes, training staff and managing customer expectations.

Once marketeers recognize that customer care is a high priority responsibility, it is likely that their impact will be of significant benefit to organizations in the service industries' sector. However, marketeers should not stop at this point, but extrapolate the marketing management process to exploit quality as a prime variable through which to build market share. This latter action can be achieved where the marketing department recognizes that the current customer care system can provide a proactive, instead of reactive, mechanism through which to build customer attitudes towards the organization.

As shown in Fig. 11.2, the customer care system can measure performance against standards, and, where variance occurs, programmes can be implemented to redesign organizational processes, to further develop employee interpersonal skills, or to introduce campaigns to revise customer expectations. The weakness of this system is that the standards are based

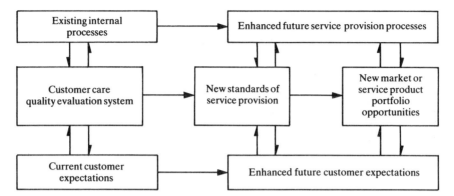

Figure 11.3 Proactive customer care development system.

upon the current market situation in terms of determining the appropriate internal or external standard of performance. Once current quality performance is found to be acceptable, the marketeer should begin to further evolve the system in order to determine any possible improvement in service levels based on higher internal efficiencies and/or new process technologies. This will then provide the basis for a new market or product service portfolio strategy (Fig. 11.3).

For example, to improve procurement, stock control and delivery times, a wholesaler has upgraded their telesales operation by installing a more powerful computerized order entry system. The data-processing department is approached by the marketing group to determine whether, by linking the system to the computer files of key customers, it is possible to improve item level sales forecasts. This move has proved successful and the wholesaler has been able to achieve a much better balance between stock on hand and customer order patterns. Although there is little difference in product range compared to competition, the wholesaler is able to build market share on the basis of a proven higher level of customer care in areas such as delivery times, minimal invoicing errors and rapid response to unexpected variation in customer order patterns.

The marketing group is now considering the possibility that the system could provide the basis for (*a*) a consultancy service advising retail customers on optimizing their store level stocking policies, (*b*) a market research company providing analysis of menu cycle trends in the catering industry and (*c*) offering to manage the food procurement activities of organizations in the health care industry.

REFERENCES

1. D. Cowell, *The Marketing of Services*, Heinemann, 1984.
2. C. Lovelock, *Service Marketing*, Prentice-Hall, 1984.

3. S. Majaro, 'Insurance, too, needs marketing' in *Marketing in Perspective*, Allen & Unwin, 1982.
4. T. Tickell, 'The charge of the plastic brigade?' *Marketing Week*, 1989.
5. J. A. Czepiel, M. R. Solomon and C. F. Surprenant, *The Service Encounter*, Lexington Books, 1985.
6. 'British Airways high ambition', *Business*, February 1989.
7. A. Hooley and D. Cowell, 'Service marketing in the UK: a survey of current practice and performance', *Service Industries Journal*, vol. 5, 1985.
8. I. Chaston, 'Marketing consumer financial services: a need to reconsider?', *Banking World*, vol. 5, No. 10, 1987.
9. I. Chaston, 'Management of the client relationship', *Accountancy*, vol. 100, No. 1131, 1987.
10. J. Driver, 'Estate agency: a marketing challenge' in *Marketing in the Service Industries*, G. Foxall (ed.), Frank Cass, 1985.
11. B. Katz, *How to Manage Customer Care*, Gower, 1987.
12. R. C. Lewis and B. H. Booms, 'The marketing aspects of service quality' in *Emerging Prospectives on Service Marketing*, L. L. Berry (ed.), American Marketing Association, 1983.
13. D. A. Collier, 'The customer service and quality challenge', *Service Industries Journal*, vol. 7, 1987.
14. I. Chaston, 'The partner as quality controller', *Accountancy*, vol. 100, No. 1142, 1988.

TWELVE
MANAGING CHANGE

THE NEED FOR CHANGE

A keystone of the marketing-orientated philosophy of management is that companies survive and grow by proactively meeting the changing requirements of their customers while concurrently overcoming new threats posed by changes in competitors' strategies. Companies who stand still are unlikely to survive.

At the interface between the company and the customer, it is the marketeer who is most likely to identify new opportunities for increased market penetration and/or diversification. However, it is not sufficient simply to recognize the need for change. As the majority of employees feel that change represents a threat to their position within the organization,[1,2] the marketeer must not only accept the responsibility for determining the need for change, but, in order to be truly effective, the individual must also be prepared to contribute to the more difficult process of managing the adoption and implementation of the proposed strategy for change.

MARINE CIRCUITS LTD

Marine Circuits was originally established to supply standard components and repair services to manufacturers and distributors of electronic equipment in the boat industry. Over recent years the company has diversified into (a) the assembly of subcomponents for other firms, (b) manufacturing and marketing of products developed by the company or produced under licence from Pacific Basin firms, and (c) participating in joint ventures with other electronics companies to create 'complete electronic system solutions' for the

Table 12.1   Financial performance by sectors (£ million)

	Components and repair services	Subassembly manufacturing	OEM and systems ventures	Total
Sales	30	30	20	80
Cost of goods	29	27	14	70
Gross profit	1	3	6	10
Operating expenses	0.5	1.5	4	6
Net profit before tax	0.5	1.5	2	4
	Net assets	20		
	ROI	20%		

marine sector of the defence industry. The organizational structure is the traditional standard function type, as shown in Fig. 12.1. The marketing director's product line responsibilities are restricted to the subassembly, OEM and joint venture systems project areas. Frank Ward, who has been with the company for many years, retains autonomous control over all aspects of managing the components and repairs operation.

Three years ago the company's financial performance by sectors was as shown by Table 12.1. At that time Frank Ward and George Hall were the instigators of a business strategy designed to double the company's sales within ten years. Their proposal was approved by the Board, and the current financial situation is shown in Table 12.2.

Andrew Howell has only been with the company for six months. He decided to analyse the financial performance over the last three years. His conclusion was that although absolute sales and net profitability have both increased, insufficient recognition has been given by his colleagues to the fact

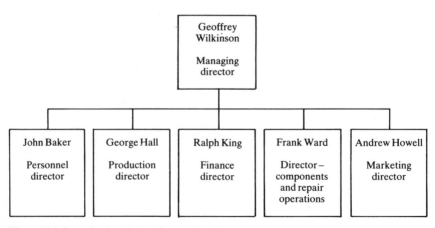

Figure 12.1 Organizational chart for Marine Circuits Ltd.

Table 12.2   Marine Circuits Ltd — current financial situation (£ million)

	Components and servicing	Subassembly manufacturing	OEMs and joing ventures	Total
Sales	40	40	24	104
Cost of goods	38.6	36.4	17.4	92.4
Gross profit	1.4	3.6	6.6	11.6
Operating expenses	0.8	1.8	4.0	6.6
Net profit before tax	0.6	1.8	2.6	5.0

Net assets	26.0
ROI	19.2%

that (*a*) net profit as a percentage of sales has declined (from 5.0 to 4.8 per cent) and (*b*) return on investment (ROI) has fallen (from 20 to 19.2 per cent). The main cause of ROI reduction is a rise in net assets, reflecting a £5m increase in the components inventory and subassembly stocks plus work-in-progress.

Preliminary discussions with Frank Ward and George Hall revealed that they saw little reason for concern. In fact, their view was that the latest financial results indicated the company was well on the path to doubling in size within ten years. Andrew realized that his was very much a minority opinion, but he felt that if the company's financial objectives were not modified, there would be a further erosion in net profitability and ROI. In these circumstances he was certain that the company's bankers would become concerned about the organization's ability to cover future interest charges and loan repayments.

GAINING ACCEPTANCE FOR THE NEED FOR CHANGE

Research on companies that fail has shown that such an outcome could probably have been avoided if senior management had accepted the need for a revision in strategy in response to changing business conditions. In theory, a change in strategy should occur because top management has identified a gap between planned and actual performance. The problem is that managers seem to exhibit a sense of inertia, burying their heads in the sand and not being prepared to question variances in performance until it is too late. Even where there is evidence of growing problems, such information tends to be ignored if it does not fit with the manager's own preconceptions. Furthermore, once a crisis occurs, managers often fall back on strategies that have been successful in the past, even though these are clearly unsuitable in the new circumstances.

Strategic blindness seems most prevalent in companies that have been major forces in an industry in the past. Executives persuade themselves that any problem is only temporary in nature and can be overcome by a small increase in expenditure or investment. Unfortunately, the net result of this attitude is that when the company does eventually fail, the size of the losses facing creditors is even larger.

The marketeer who advocates a change in strategy has a long and difficult battle to fight. It will be necessary to persuade others to revise their attitudes even before the topic of changing strategies can be accepted as a legitimate topic of conversation. Even if other managers can be persuaded to re-examine their beliefs, there will be further battles to be fought in gaining agreement on a new strategy, obtaining adequate resources to support new marketing plans, and persuading employees at all levels in the organization to modify working practices.

Defenders of existing strategies usually outnumber those who advocate change. Furthermore, these defenders are unlikely to submit easily. At best they will be seen by others as having made a mistake and at worst could lose their jobs. Hence, through both covert and/or overt actions, the defenders will use every possible weapon available to discredit or undermine the position of the seekers of change.[3, 4]

UNDERSTANDING THE DEFENDERS

To have any chance of overcoming resistance to change among the defenders of current strategies, the marketeer must understand the underlying approach to the opposition's position. It is likely that this will fall into one of the following categories:

- *Rejecters of logic.* These individuals are unwilling to even consider that the current strategy might be invalid. They will argue from the perspective that there is insufficient evidence for any change at this point in time. Their viewpoint can be based upon a genuine difference of opinion in the interpretation of the evidence presented to support a need for change. Unfortunately to defend their position, they may be willing to reject indications of a developing problem on the grounds that any downturn in performance is a short-term aberration. The company may have to be on the verge of collapse before the rejecters of logic are willing to entertain any doubts about the wisdom of current strategies.
- *Accepters of logic.* These individuals are willing to support the proposition of a need for change, but cannot be convinced that the new strategy is appropriate. Rejection of the solution may be based upon an opinion that there is a better solution and/or that the proposed solution

will divert resources away from other activities that they believe to be more important.

● *Rejecters on principle.* This type of rejection is to be found among those who evaluate any solution in relation to its potential impact upon their future role in the organization. This form of rejection is the one that has been most thoroughly researched during studies on the management of change.

It is natural for most people to react to any new situation by considering how they personally will be affected by the proposed change.[5, 6] Unless they immediately perceive that such change is to their benefit, the natural response is to reject the proposition because it could leave them worse off in the future. There are a number of possible interpretations of how they would be adversely affected by change. Possibly they see that their skills would be rendered obsolete. Alternatively, new skills will be required and they are uncertain of their abilities to acquire these. There may also be concern about being placed in a new group and having to develop new working relationships in the workforce. Another common cause of concern is that job security will be threatened by redundancy, transfer to a new location, or loss of authority.

GAINING SUPPORT FOR A PROPOSAL OF CHANGE

When a strategy has been in place for some years, a coalition of support will have evolved. Unless the group question the validity of perpetuating the current strategy, an individual who holds a different opinion will have a difficult time gaining acceptance for the need for change. In these circumstances, the marketeer who holds a minority opinion will have to identify ways of persuading others to agree with that individual's position. This process will have to continue until sufficient support has been generated to enable the marketeer to form an alternative coalition that is strong enough to overcome opposition.

Attracting others to a cause may be achieved through education. The marketeer may provide information that will cause others to question their current viewpoint because they begin to accept the merits of a superior argument. When other managers perceive a risk associated with the new concept, it may be necessary to offer incentives to weaken their resistance. The incentives will usually involve defining the benefits to the individual should the new strategy be adopted (e.g., increased authority; prospects for promotion).

Once a reasonable level of support has been achieved, it is likely that a committee will be formed to assess the strengths and weaknesses of the new proposal. The creation of the committee will make it legitimate for managers to discuss openly the issues associated with the proposed change. If there is going to be continued opposition, however, the formation of the committee will probably be seen as the signal for open warfare by the defenders of the current strategy.

MARINE CIRCUITS — STRATEGIC CHANGE

Andrew Howell felt that the prime objective for the company should be to improve both profitability and ROI. His examination of the situation led him to conclude that this could be achieved by restricting plans for sales growth to the higher margin OEM products and joint ventures while, at the same time, cutting back sales on components, servicing and subassembly work. The emphasis on decreasing sales should be in the components sector because this would reduce the company's need to hold large inventories of such items. The consequent shrinkage in components would reduce net assets, increase ROI and lower the company's borrowing requirements.

To gain acceptance for the new strategy Andrew would have to convince the managing director and other directors. Through his understanding of these individuals, it was possible to forecast their reaction to his proposals as follows:

- Geoffrey Wilkinson, the managing director, would probably accept the logic but reject the proposed solution as his earlier successes in the company were based upon building up the components and servicing activities.
- George Hall would reject the logic of the proposal on the grounds that he assisted in the development of the company's existing business strategy.
- Frank Ward would reject the logic of the proposal because the revised plan would endanger his role and status within the organization.
- Ralph King and John Baker would both accept the new strategy as long as they could avoid being in conflict with other members of the management team.

It is apparent that to obtain support for his position, Andrew will have to gain acceptance for his ideas from Geoffrey Wilkinson and George Hall. George's support is vital because only he has the expertise to know whether it is feasible to increase sales for manufactured products. As George has always indicated a willingness to accept concepts if they would strengthen his position in the company, Andrew felt that an incentive approach of needing to expand the company's manufacturing operation would appeal to him.

Andrew arranged to have lunch with George and, without revealing any concerns about profitability, raised the issue of the practicalities of expanding the OEM manufacturing operation. George indicated that this was possible as long as additional financial resources were made available to support the hiring of more design engineers and plant operatives.

Geoff Wilkinson had always seemed very open-minded about other proposals that Andrew had made. Andrew therefore felt that an education approach could be used to obtain the managing director's acceptance of the revised strategy. He submitted a confidential report, which highlighted the profit implications of sustaining the current strategy and described the potential benefits of expanding sales for OEM products. The managing director's reaction was to request that Andrew form a small working party with George Hall and Ralph King. The managing director considered that their input would be vital because of the implications on plant capacity and/or capital expenditure to handle any additional output of OEM product.

Andrew was pleased to find that Geoff Wilkinson was perceptive enough to recognize Frank Ward's potential opposition. He suggested that at this stage the working party should only examine the practicalities of expanding OEM sales and avoid any discussion of the second phase of the revised strategy involving de-emphasis of sales for components and subassembly work.

RESOLVING CONFLICT

It is usually impossible to introduce change without creating conflict as managers seek to retain their current span of authority within the organization. The conflict will not just occur during the planning phase, but will continue on as new policies are introduced that modify, alter or abolish existing working practices throughout the organization. In order to minimize conflict, marketeers will have to use a variety of approaches if new strategies are to be successfully implemented. One of the commonest approaches to conflict management is to act 'coercively', where employees are told to accept change and that any resistance could mean job losses or reduced promotional prospects. In some circumstances the employees do not believe these threats, and it may be necessary to actually fire a few individuals to persuade the workforce that the management is serious about introducing new working practices. The major risk of a coercive approach is that it will exacerbate employees' resentment to the company's revised policies. Nevertheless, in situations where speed of action is essential (e.g., without change, the company will go bankrupt), and the changes are known to be unpopular, then coercion may be the best option to manage conflict.

Where time permits, however, it is clearly preferable to use a more participative approach. By involving employees in the change process at the earliest possible point, the greater is the likelihood that they will react positively. For the participative approach to be effective, management should provide detailed information on both the need for, and the logic behind the proposed changes. But this process will only be effective where the marketeer has already established a relationship of trust with the audience to whom the information will be delivered.

In this approach, communication of any type is presented in a form that permits a two-way dialogue in which the recipients of the information are provided with an opportunity to ask questions or propose alternative solutions. When subordinates can clearly understand the reasons for the rejection of any of their suggestions, it is more probable that they will accept the manager's original proposals. If a marketeer indicates an interest in receiving comments from subordinates, it is vital that the subordinates believe this to be a participative dialogue and not a manager just paying lip service to the concept of participative discussions.

The participative approach is unlikely to be productive in an atmosphere of widespread fear and anxiety (real or imagined) about a proposed change. In these circumstances the marketeer should attempt to be supportive and spend time understanding the underlying causes of the fears being expressed by subordinates. In many instances this type of discussions can be used to introduce the issues of the new skills that will have to be acquired by subordinates before they can effectively execute their revised job roles.

Another mechanism for resolving conflict can be to offer incentives to reduce opposition. This method will usually involve negotiations during which the two parties are willing to modify their stance in return for additional benefits. An example would be an agreement to modify work practices in return for a bonus based on higher productivity. In those situations where subordinates are members of a union, this organization will often provide a full-time official to negotiate on behalf of the workforce.

Sometimes one can use the mechanism of co-option to resolve conflict. This approach involves the inclusion of individuals in the planning or implementation phase in return for an endorsement of the proposed change. The risk associated with this method is that the co-opted individuals assume that their opinion is actually important. At the point when they recognize the fallacy of this assumption, a common reaction is to covertly oppose the change process. Their ability to succeed in this action is aided by the fact that through co-option they have gained access to confidential information. Hence co-option, although popular, is not usually very effective. Where an individual is frequently seen to use this approach, subordinates become very wary of the manager and endeavour to minimize contact in order to avoid being drawn into the change process.

No marketeer can expect to identify a single approach that can be applied to every conflict resolution situation. It is, therefore, important to examine the specific circumstances of any situation and then determine which is the most appropriate mechanism to be used. A continuum of choices is available ranging from coercion at one extreme to an extensively participative approach at the other. Where the marketeer faces massive resistance, a participative style is more likely to succeed than a dictatorial one. This is especially true where the individual is completely dependent upon the wholehearted cooperation of subordinates when implementing a proposed change in work practices.

Where the marketeer expects minimal resistance, or the change has little impact on the majority of the staff, coercion will prove quite feasible. When the risks are high or an immediate change is necessary, then this is also a situation where coercion should be used. Coercion is also mandatory where the initiator has little power over others. Although this may at first appear illogical, only marketeers who have already established a high level of authority over others are able to tolerate a participative approach when managing change.[7]

MARINE CIRCUITS — HANDLING OPPOSITION

Andrew already recognized that Frank Ward represented the most likely source of opposition. The creation of the working party was certain to be the signal for open warfare over changing the company strategy. After some reflection on this fact, Andrew raised his concerns with Geoff Wilkinson. Wilkinson agreed that, before the working party was formed, it would be necessary to review the situation with Frank. Geoff's previous experience led him to conclude that a coercive approach would be required and that he, as managing director, should initiate a discussion with Frank. Furthermore, he would make it clear at this meeting that the working party had his support for examining the concept of expanding the OEM operation.

Andrew was then able to brief the other two members of the working party, knowing that for the moment Frank's opposition had been neutralized. Given the differing expertise of the working party, Andrew decided to use a very participative approach in the analysis of the proposed changes in strategy. Their deliberations over a four-week period validated Andrew's proposals and a formal presentation to the complete senior management was scheduled.

As expected, Frank Ward was extremely critical and focused upon the fact that Andrew's limited experience of the marine electronics industry was the reason for reaching an incorrect conclusion about the future direction for the company. These comments were received with some sympathy by John Baker and Geoff Wilkinson. Sensing victory, Frank suggested that the new strategy be shelved and possibly re-examined in a 'couple of years' time'. At this point both George Hall and Ralph King made it clear that their involvement in the working party had caused them to completely accept the need for an immediate change in strategy. This very positive new coalition eventually caused everyone except Frank to adopt the new strategy of expanding the OEM operation with a concurrent reduction in the components and the subassembly operations.

IMPLEMENTING THE CHANGE

Developing and gaining approval for the change process plan may not be easy but the marketeer can expect the implementation phase to be just as problematic — if not more so. In fact, studies often reveal that although a company may have adopted an appropriate strategy, the marketing department then fails to manage the implementation of the new plan.[8, 9]

Research on strategy-implementation problems has shown that the top ten causes of failure, ranked in descending order of importance, are:[10]

1. Implementation took more time than was originally allocated.
2. Major problems surfaced during implementation that had not been identified beforehand.
3. Coordination of implementation activities was inadequate.
4. Competing activities and crises distracted attention from the implementation process.
5. Capability of employees was not sufficient.
6. Training and instructions given to subordinates were not adequate.
7. Uncontrollable factors in the external environment had an adverse impact.
8. Leadership and direction were not adequate.
9. Key implementation tasks were not clearly defined.
10. Information systems to monitor implementation were not adequate.

The marketeer involved in an implementation failure might be forgiven if the cause was an uncontrollable external event (e.g., a manufacturer of vehicle-cleaning equipment who launches a new product line for garage forecourts just as the Government instigates a drought order forbidding the washing of vehicles). But all the other reasons for failure are attributable to the simple fact that the marketeer was an ineffective manager.

THE MARKETEER AS A MANAGER

Until the seventies, the accepted definition of the key tasks of the manager was that of planning, directing and controlling. It was therefore assumed that as long as managers had acquired expertise in their prime functional area (e.g., product development or promotional planning) and were provided with adequate information systems, all would be well. Unfortunately, this philosophy ignored the fact that managing involves working with others and being responsible for subordinates. People in an organization can offer loyalty, support and cooperation. However, these same individuals, as they are members of the human race, can be irritable, irresponsible, disloyal and obstructive. Staff within marketing departments are no exception to this rule. Research has demonstrated that the ability of a marketeer to succeed will depend heavily upon having acquired a very high level of interpersonal skills.[11]

Over the last two decades studies by behavioural scientists have led to a much fuller understanding of the role of managers and the mechanisms available to improve their effectiveness in the vital area of working with others. A leading researcher in management behaviour, H. Mintzberg, has proposed ten roles (or 'organized sets of behaviour') for the manager.[12] Three of the roles — figurehead, leader and liaison — involve working within and outside of the work team to ensure tasks are agreed and understood. This will require an ability to fulfil the information provision roles of monitor, disseminator and spokesperson of the group for which the marketeer is responsible. The group can only discharge its responsibilities if the marketeer also effectively fulfils the other four roles of entrepreneur, problem solver, resource allocator and negotiator.

THE MARKETEER AS AN EFFECTIVE MANAGER

In order to be effective managers, marketeers will need to appreciate which of the ten roles should receive priority in relation to their position in the organization and the nature of the marketing programmes for which their groups are responsible. The organization should not expect a marketeer, when assigned to a new area of responsibility, to understand intuitively the relative importance of the ten roles. Guidance must be provided on matters such as boundaries of responsibility, degree of authority over others, scale of resources available and the degree of autonomy over how such resources can be utilized.

In addition to the provision of this knowledge, the company should ensure that marketeers have acquired skills in the areas of motivating subordinates, communication and delegation. As people are rarely born with an innate ability to manage others, expertise will need to be developed through the use of performance appraisal and training systems. Unfortunately, compared to Pacific Basin countries, many companies in the western world do not invest sufficient funds in the training and development of their staff.[13] It should therefore come as no surprise to those organizations to find that their ability to respond effectively to new competitive threats is severely hampered by the inadequate managerial abilities of their marketing staff.

This lack of investment in staff development programmes is further evidenced by the results of research on the training of marketing executives in the UK.[14] The study revealed that over the three-year period 1983–1986, almost one-third of the 2000 respondents had not received any training. Of the remainder, the average participation in training schemes was only three days per year. On the issue of awareness of the need for more training, 35 per cent of respondents felt they had not received sufficient training to succeed in their current job role. Furthermore, over 70 per cent of respondents considered that they had not received sufficient training to achieve their planned career goals.

Therefore, any organization wishing to ensure that the marketing department is capable of managing the process of implementing change, must review the current staff appraisal and management development systems. Although there is general acceptance of this requirement, there is still a widespread tendency to treat the planning of human resources and the management of business strategies as two quite separate issues.[15] As more knowledge has been accumulated on the implementation of change, however, it is becoming increasingly apparent that success is dependent upon integrating these two areas of the management process.[16]

ORGANIZATIONAL CULTURE

Although integration of management activities appears to be a relatively simple objective, achievement of this goal will often prove difficult. To a major degree this is because integration of any function or process can only occur if it is perceived as compatible with the value system of the organization. Norms and attitudes which, collectively, form the basis of the values of an organization are commonly known as 'organizational culture'. This culture provides the meaning and direction that mobilizes the organization into action. Whether such action is beneficial or detrimental will depend upon the prevailing culture being compatible with the mission of the organization and the style of leadership provided by the management team.[17]

Despite some claims to the contrary, it is now accepted that there is no one single 'best' organizational culture. What is important, however, is that the prevailing culture is used to reinforce the objectives, strategies and management policies of the organization. A vital task for the marketeers seeking to achieve managerial excellence is to ensure that the prevailing norms and values of the organization are supportive of the processes associated with optimizing the relationships between market opportunities and internal corporate capabilities. For a company in a rapidly changing market environment, the culture will probably need to be biased towards flexibility, adaptability and innovative approaches to problem-solving. In contrast, in the transition of market state from growth to maturity, there may be the requirement for a culture which places emphasis on taking a rational, more controlled, less impulsive attitude towards management processes in order to optimize the productivity of corporate assets.

Modifying an existing culture, or attempting to introduce a new culture, is possibly the most complex of all of the management tasks. For marketeers to be accepted as being capable of contributing towards this activity, they must first establish an image of competency in their primary role of managing the marketing process. Achievement of this goal will involve the utilization of the concepts and techniques of the type presented in this text. Once the marketeer has demonstrated a high degree of professionalism, the importance of the marketing role will be accepted by other members of the organization. Only at that stage will senior management be able to draw upon the expertise of the marketeer to assist in sustaining the culture most appropriate to the organization's long-term strategic goals.

REFERENCES

1. R. James, *Corporate Strategy and Change—The Management of People*, University of Chicago Press, 1978.
2. J. B. Quinn, 'Managing strategic change', *Sloan Management Review*, vol. 21, No. 4, Summer 1980.
3. J. P. Kotter and L. A. Schlesinger, 'Choosing strategies for change', *Harvard Business Review*, March 1979.
4. R. A. Johnston, F. E. Kurst and J. E. Roseweig, *People and Systems*, McGraw-Hill, 1967.
5. M. West and J. Hughes, 'Lessons from experiences', *International Journal of Manpower*, vol. 1/2, 1983.
6. A. D. Zoltmann and R. Duncan, *Strategies for Planned Change*, Harper & Row, 1977.
7. J. B. Quinn, 'Managing innovation: controlled chaos', *Harvard Business Review*, May 1985.
8. K. Deveney, 'Colgate puts the squeeze on Crest', *Business Week*, August 1985.
9. R. F. Hartley, *Marketing Mistakes*, 4th edn., Wiley, 1989.
10. L. D. Alexander, 'Successfully implementing strategic decisions', *Long Range Planning*, vol. 18, No. 3, 1985.
11. A. Ventatesh and D. L. Wileman, 'Interpersonal influence in product management', *Journal of Marketing*, vol. 40, 1976.
12. H. Mintzberg, *The Nature of Management Work*, Harper & Row, 1973.
13. Coopers and Lybrand Associates, *A Challenge to Complacency: changing attitudes to training*, Manpower Services Commission, November 1985.
14. Plymouth Business School, 'The background and training of marketing executives', consolidated report for the Institute of Marketing, November 1987.
15. 'Wanted, a manager to fit each strategy', *Business Week*, February 1980.
16. R. H. Kilmann, *Beyond the Quick Fix*, Jossey-Bass, 1987.
17. R. H. Kilmann, M. J. Saxton and R. Serpa, *Gaining Control of the Corporate Culture*, Jossey-Bass, 1985.

GLOSSARY

Advertising Any form of non-personal promotion paid for by the sponsor and usually delivered via media such as television or print.

Agents Independent individuals or firms that represent another organization and receive commission on sales generated.

Annual plan A plan produced annually by an organization.

Assets Resources of the organization that are capable of providing benefits and can be valued in monetary terms.

Attitudes Emotional evaluations of belief that indicate intensity of feelings.

Awareness Level of knowledge about a situation, product or service.

Balance sheet A list of assets of an organization and the claims against it.

Benefit The requirement the customer seeks from a product.

Boston Consulting Group (BCG) The organization which developed the cash cow/dog/rising star/problem child planning matrix concept.

Brand Specific name given to a product to assist identification by the customer.

Break even The point at which revenues equal costs.

Budget The amount of money to be spent on a specific activity.

Buffer stocks Inventory levels maintained in reserve to meet unexpected demand (also known as 'safety stocks').

Business analysis Estimation of market opportunity and potential profitability.

Capital The owner's claim against a business.

Capital budgeting Analytical technique to evaluate cost of capital over time.

Capital investment The amount of capital that will be required to fund a project.

Cash cow Product with high market share in a low growth market.

Cash flow Flow of funds in and out of a business.

Channel of distribution Network of organizations involved in moving goods from the producer to the final customer.

Communication channel Pathway through which marketing information is distributed.

Competition Organizations competing with the firm for business.

Competitive advantage An advantage a firm can offer over competing firms.

Competitive conditions Variables describing the intensity and nature of rivals' strategies and tactics.

Computer-aided design (CAD) The use of computer systems to design products.

Computer-aided manufacturing (CAM) The use of computers to assist in the manufacturing process.

Computer numerical control (CNC) The use of computer systems to control the settings on equipment such as machine tools.

Concept testing Assessing potential reaction by customers to a new idea.

Consumer behaviour The behaviour consumers exhibit in considering a purchase or responding to a firm's marketing programmes.

Consumer buying process The process whereby the consumer reaches a purchase decision.

Core market system Those components of the industry market system, such as suppliers, producers, intermediaries and end-user outlets, that provide the structure through which customers can obtain products.

Cost-benefit analysis An analysis based on the relationship between benefit and the cost of providing the benefit.

Coupon A direct-response device for providing the customer with a temporary discount or added value.

Customer care The provision of an adequate quality of service to customers.

Demand curve A curve describing the relationship between quantity and price.

Demographics A measurement of age, income, education and other related characteristics of a population in a market.

Direct distribution A producer that sells output to final customers without involving any intermediaries.

Direct mail Promotion of products through mailing promotional information to the final customer.

Direct marketing All of the marketing processes designed to gain a response from the final customer.

Directional policy matrix A planning tool to determine appropriate strategies in relation to market opportunity and corporate capability.

Discontinuation Removal of a product from the market.

Discount pricing Pricing at a reduced level to stimulate sales.

Distributors Intermediaries linking producer and customer.

Diversification Entry into new areas of business.

Dog A product with a low share in a low-growth market.

Economic order quantity (EOQ) The amount of units that should be ordered to maintain the most economical level of stocks.

Economy of scale The benefit of reduced total costs by operating on a larger scale.

Entry strategy Strategy for entering a new market.

Environment The conditions, both within and external to the company, that can have influence over corporate performance.

Environmental analysis Examination of the variables in an environment.

Excess capacity Having production capacity greater than needed to supply demand.

Expansion strategy A strategy of increasing market share.

Experience curve Curve reflecting decreasing costs of production as the organization increases output and gains experience of business processes.

Fast moving consumer goods (FMCG) Used to describe larger organizations in major consumer markets.

Financial analysis An analysis to determine the financial aspects of a situation.

Fixed assets Those assets intended to be held to generate profit rather than to be used in day-to-day revenue generation activities.

Fixed costs Those costs which do not vary as company trading activities change.

Focus groups Groups of individuals that are interviewed together for market research purposes.

Forecast An estimate of the future value of some variable or the occurrence of an event.

Free offer Free items offered as an inducement to purchase.

Frequency How often a target market is exposed to a promotional message.

Generic product A type or class of product designed to satisfy an area of need.

Geographic segmentation Subdivision of a market into geographic areas as the basis for focusing marketing activities.

Global marketing Marketing using identical products across all countries.

Goals The measurable statement of objectives to be achieved by a strategy and/or plan.

Gross national product (GNP) The total value of all goods and services produced in a country in a year.

Growth strategy A strategy designed to increase sales in either existing and/or new markets.

Historical data Information obtained from prior activities.

Homogeneous markets Markets in which customer needs are very similar.

Horizontal diversification Entry into new market areas in the same level of the market system.

Idea generation The process of generating new product ideas.

Image The mental picture that the customer holds about a product or organization.

Implementation process The process through which plans are carried out.

Independent retailers Retail operations not affiliated with other units in the same area of business.

Industry attractiveness A measurement used to describe the scale of market opportunity.

Industry potential An estimate of total future sales opportunity.

In-store activities The promotional activities associated with marketing at store level.

Intermediaries Specialist organizations who are involved in managing channels of distribution.

Intrapreneurship An entrepreneurial spirit within large organizations.

Introduction stage The first phase of the life of a product.

IT Abbreviation for Information Technology, describing the processes associated with the use of computers to process information.

Inventory A quantity of materials, supplies or finished goods maintained to balance supply and demand (alternative description, 'stock').

Inventory holding costs The costs associated with holding inventory.

Inventory turnover A measurement of the flow of items through the inventory.

Joint venture Where two or more companies agree to work together on a project.

Just in time (JIT) Method of managing supplies to minimize inventory costs.

Liabilities Financial obligations of the firm.

Licensing Agreeing to the use of technology or knowledge by a third party in return for a fee or royalty.

Lifestyle Everyday behavioural orientation of a group of people covering such facets as activities, feeling, attitudes and opinions.

Lifestyle segmentation Segmentation of a market on the basis of lifestyles, (alternative description, psychographic segmentation).

Line extension Process of broadening product range by adding new products usually of a similar nature as that of existing products.

Macroenvironment The general business environment outside the core market containing such influencing variables as economic conditions and political or social trends.

Management culture The shared values of the management within an organization.

Management information system (MIS) A structured interaction between personnel, procedures and data storage systems to provide information to assist decision-making.

Margin The difference between price and costs or revenue and costs.

Market development Generation of revenue by exploiting new sales opportunities.

Market growth The rate at which sales are increasing in a market.

Market leader The organization that has the highest share of total market sales.

Market segment A part of a total market that has a measurable commonality.

Market segmentation A strategy by which the market is broken down into submarkets, and specialist strategies are directed at each segment.

Market share The proportion of sales achieved by a firm in a market.

Market testing The process by which new products are evaluated prior to launch.

Marketing The process of utilizing the marketing mix to satisfy customer needs.

Marketing decision support systems (MDSS) The application of computer-based information acquisition and processing systems to aid the marketing management decision process.

Marketing environment The surroundings in which the organization operates its marketing activities.

Marketing information system The information system used by the managers of the marketing operation.

Marketing management The activities associated with identifying market needs, developing an appropriate strategy and implementing a plan to achieve the objectives of the organization.

Marketing mix The combination and allocation of resources in the areas of product, price, promotion and distribution.

Marketing planning The process of developing a marketing plan.

Marketing research The structured process whereby information is generated to assist the marketing decision activities of the organization.

Marketing system The group of interacting and interdependent variables that constitute the market of which the firm is a member.

Mass marketing A concept whereby the same product is made available to all customers in the market.

Media The channels used to deliver advertising messages.

Mission A statement that establishes the general direction an organization intends to take in the market.

Multinational A large commercial organization operating across a number of major markets around the world.

New product development The process of taking an idea from conception through to launch into the market.

New product plan The marketing plan for a new product.

Niche A specialist sector of demand in a market.

Niching The strategy of satisfying specialist demand in a sector of the market.

Objectives Definition of an organization's intended achievements, usually encompassing a statement over financial performance.

Operations research (OR) The application of mathematical and statistical models to determine appropriate management decisions.

Order entry system Process whereby an organization accepts customer orders.

Original Equipment Manufacturers (OEM) The organization responsible for the manufacture of a piece of equipment (e.g., the Ford Motor Company as an OEM making cars; IBM as a producer of computers)

Out-of-stock Phrase describing the situation when an organization has no goods available for sale.

Overdraft Method of borrowing short-terms funds from a bank.

Overheads Costs of operating a business which cannot be directly allocated to a specific production process.

Overhead absorption Allocation of overhead costs to the total cost of manufacturing a product.

Own label Description of products marketed under the name of a firm, usually an intermediary, other than that of the original producer (alternative description, 'private label').

Packaging The function of enclosing the product for both distribution and promotional purposes.

Penetration pricing Pricing at a lower than usual level to gain rapid entry into a market.

Perceived value The value of a product to the customer.

Personal interview A market research technique using face-to-face meetings to collect information.

Physical distribution The process of moving and storing goods from the time of production until sale to the final customer.

Positioning The strategy by which the product is positioned relative to other products in the market in the minds of the potential customers.

Price competition The use of price as the main mechanism to build sales or defend the firm from competitors.

Price pack Special promotional pack sold at lower than usual price.

Price-value relationship The relationship between price charged and the value of the product as perceived by the customer.

Pricing The action whereby the price to be charged is determined by the organization.

Primary research The collection of new market information by research.

Problem children Products with a low market share in a rapidly growing market.

Product differentiation The strategy by which the company's product is seen to be different from other products in the market.

Product extension Process of lengthening the life of a product.

Product lifecycle (PLC) The stages of a product, from introduction to growth, maturity and decline.

Product line Range of products offered by a company.

Profit The excess of revenues over expenses.

Profitability The level of profit being generated by a firm.

Profit impact of marketing strategy (PIMS) A research programme that generates data bases on relationships between strategies and performance.

Promotion Activities associated with the provision of information to the market; includes activities such as advertising, personal selling, sales promotions and publicity.

Promotional discounts Short-term, temporary reduction in price to stimulate customer purchase behaviour.

Promotional expenditure The amount of money expended on promotional activity.

Publicity Non-paid and non-personal promotion, very often involving mention of the promotional message in the media.

Purchase decision The decision made by the customer to buy the product.

Reach The proportion of the market that will be covered by a promotional message.

Recall A means of measuring the proportion of the population who remember a promotional campaign.

Repeat purchase The purchase of a product on a regular basis.

Repositioning Changing the positioning of a product relative to a competitor's products or other products in the company's product line.

Research and development (R&D) The activities associated with acquiring information and the understanding of technological or scientific processes.

Retailer A channel intermediary who sells the product to the final customer.

Return on investment (ROI)   Profit performance expressed as a rate of return on the assets employed by the firm (alternative description, 'rate of return on capital employed').

Reverse growth   Reducing the size of the business through decreasing the total volume of sales.

Sales forecast   Estimate of sales in a specified period of time.

Salesforce   The individuals responsible for the personal selling process.

Sales promotion   A non-personal form of promotion usually designed to generate trial and repeat by a temporary offer of greater value (e.g. reduced price, participation in a competition).

Scenario planning   A planning technique involving the development of assumptions about future market conditions.

Screening   The evaluation stage of the new product development process when products are still at the ideas phase.

Secondary research   The market research process involving acquisition of information from existing sources.

Selling   The promotional process of face-to-face negotiation with the customer.

Service   An intangible product.

Service marketing   The processes associated with the marketing of services.

Star   A high share product in a rapidly growing market.

Strategic management   The process of selecting the most appropriate approach by which an organization can be successful.

Strategy   The method by which an organization can achieve specified objectives.

Subsidiaries   Organizations controlled by another, usually larger, organization.

SWOT   Acronym for a planning technique to evaluate the strengths, weaknesses, opportunities and threats facing an organization.

Tactics   Actions taken to implement a strategy.

Target margin   The desired profit to be achieved per unit sold.

Target market   A definable group of customers to whom a product will be marketed.

Telesales   The use of telephone selling to market products (alternative description, 'Telemarketing')

Timing   The sequencing of a plan or decided action.

Total quality management (TQM)   Philosophy of ensuring all members of an organization are committed to delivering a required level of quality.

Trial   The first ever purchase of a product by the customer.

Variable costs   Costs that vary in direct relation to business activity.

Vehicle   A specific media channel selected to deliver a promotion.

Vertical integration   Combination under single ownership of two or more levels of a market system.

Warehousing   Storage of goods during the distribution process.

Work-in-progress   Stocks of partly finished goods held by the manufacturer.

Working capital   The excess of current assets over current liabilities.

INDEX

Advertising, 73, 85–6, 90
Advertising expenditure models, 89–90, 101–2
Affordability budgeting, 99
Airline service image, 141–2
Alternative strategies, 49
Asset management, 102–5
Attribute listing, 61
Average projection forecast, 93
Avon Corporation, 69

Balance sheet performance, 102–5
Bank service image, 143–4
Bankers, attitudes of, 36
Barclays Bank, 74
Base technology, 34
Batch production, 33
Booz Allen, 56
Boston Consulting Group (BCG), 44
  product portfolio mix, 42–6
Brainstorming, 61
Brand awareness, 66
Break-even analysis, 123–4
British Leyland, 72
Brymor Ltd, 50–2
Business acquisitions, 58–9
Buyer behaviour, 83

CNC machines, 27, 45
Capacity planning, 133–7
Cash cow, 44
Cash dogs, 44, 46
Causal model forecasts, 94

Change, rejection responses, 154–5
  support for, 155–6
Coercion management, 157, 159
Competition, 17–8
Competitive spending analysis, 98–100
Computer models, 101–2
Concept development, 54
Conflict management, 8–9, 157–60
Control:
  diagnostic systems, 109–16
  integrative systems, 116–7
  limited systems, 108–9
  periodic systems, 108–9
  proactive systems, 117–9
  variance analysis, 108–9
Control systems, attitudes to, 107–8
Co-option to support change, 158
Corporate capability, 46–50
Cost leadership defence, 71
Cost-of-goods analysis, 123–4
Cost/benefit analysis, 99
Costs:
  fixed, 124–6
  variable, 124–6
Counter-offensive tactics, 73–4
Cross-impact forecasting, 96
Customer care: 144–9
  standards, 145–7
  variables, 145
Customers, 14–7
Cyclical sales situations, 94

De-engineering, 45

Decision support systems, 117–9
Defence tactics, 70–4
Delphi technique, 96
Demographic trends, 15
Depreciated asset scenario, 34
Designing defence systems, 70–1
Directional strategy matrix, 47–52
Distribution chain dominance, 18
Distribution channels, 19, 86–9
Distribution strategies, 86–7
Division tree technique, 61
Downstream coupling, 58
Dulux paint, 66

Econometric model, 90, 94
Economic Order Quantity (EOQ),
   126–7
Effective managerial skills, 161–2
Encirclement attack, 68–9
Environmental turbulence, 21–3
Excess capacity situations, 135–7
Experience curve, 130–3
Exponential smoothing, 93

Financial capability, 30–3
Financial services marketing, 143–4
Financial variance analysis, 113–5
Financial variance control, 111
Flank attacks, 67–8
Fmcg versus service markets, 143–5
Ford, Henry, 40
Ford versus General Motors, 40
Forecasting accuracy, 97
Forecasting sales, 93–5
Frontal assault, 65
 failures, 66
Futuribles forecasting, 96

GEC Corporation, 68
Gillette Company, 71
Guerilla warfare, 69–70

Haines Corporation versus L'Eggs,
   88–9
Handling opposing views, 159–60
High-volume production, 33
Hofmeister lager, 66
Homogeneous demand, 40
Humble Products, 3–6

IBM defence tactics, 72
Idea generation, 57
Image of production staff, 121–2
Imagery, 62

Implementing change, 160
Industrial laser market, 33
Innovation, barriers to, 56–7
 management, 55–60
Intermediaries, 18–20
Intuitive thinking, 60–2

Japanese management, 14, 17, 21
Just in time (JIT), 127–8

Kelloggs Super Noodles, 89
Key technology, 34
Kodak, 55

Laker Airlines, 32
Leapfrog attack, 69
Levi Strauss, 71
Liquidity, 103
Logical thinking, 60

MIS, 23, 115–6
Macroenvironment, 13
Management accounting, 111–6
Management decision support, 117
Managerial capability, 35–6
Managerial roles, 160–3
Managing change, 151–163
Managing information, 23, 62
Manufacturing capability, 33–4
Manufacturing capacity and ROI,
   104–5
Manufacturing management, 121–137
Marine Circuits Ltd, 151–3, 156, 159
Market defence tactics, 70–4
Market leadership, 38–40
Market segmentation, 14, 41
Market size analysis, 109–111
Market size forecast, 92–7
Market specialization, 41
Market structure/PLC policy, 86
Market systems, 13–4
Marketeers image among others, 3
Marketing expenditure, 97–100
 budget, 97–100
 control, 97–100
Marketing goals, 8
Marketing mix, 27, 76
 assessment, 89
Marketing-orientation, 1–2
Marketing/production relations, 121–3,
   129–133
Marketing role, 7
Marketing strategies, 38–46
Marketing task, 6–8

Marketing tactics, 65–74
Matrix analysis, 60
Mature market, 44
Mercury Communications, 68
Mintzberg H., 161
Mobile defence, 71
Model building, 100–2
Morphological forecasting, 96

National Westminster Bank, 74
New product activity types, 56
New product forecasting, 95
New product forecast models, 95
New product management, 53–63
Non-confrontational attack, 67–70

OEM, 27, 45
Office of innovation network, 55
OPEC, 20
Order size management, 126–7
Organizing for new products, 58–9
Organizational barriers, 56
Organizational culture, 162–3
Orion Ltd, 30–2
Overhead absorption of costs, 124–6

PIMS study, 38–9
Pacer technology, 34
Perceived quality, 79, 141–7
Percentage of sales budgeting, 99
Perestroika, 21
Performance control, 107–119
Performance indicators, 10–11
Personal selling, 85–6
Peters and Waterman, 2
Place, 29
Place dominant scenario, 29–30
Planning ROI objectives, 104–5
Plant investment decisions, 135–7
Porter M. E., 17
Position/distribution matrix, 87
Price, 28, 77–80
  cost orientated, 77
  premium, 78
  skimming, 78
  value pricing, 78
  penetration, 78
  war, 72
Price dominant scenario, 27–8
Price pack, 72, 80–2
  promotion, 82
Price preference curves, 80–1
Price/performance matrix, 130
Price/quality matrix, 78

Pricing decisions, 77–80
  strategies, 78–9
Problem children, 45
Problem-solving, innovative, 60–2
Product, 27
Product development process, 53–5
Product development programmes,
  130–3
Product discontinuation, 48–9
Product dominant scenario, 27
Product improvement programmes, 129
Product lifecycle (PLC), 42–6, 53, 86,
  129
Promotion, 28, 83–6
Promotion dominant scenario, 28–9
Promotion/price matrix, 84
Promotional channels, 83–6
Promotional funds, allocation of,
  98–102
Promotional mix, 85–6
Promotional planning, 83–6

Qualcast lawnmowers, 74
Quality of service products, 144–9
Quality problem management, 147

R&D capability, 34
Regression forecasting, 94
Retail stock management, 88
Return on investment (ROI), 38, 102–5
Rising star, 44
Rolls Royce cars, 71

SWOT, 26
Sales management models, 101
Sales promotion, 80–1
Sales response curves, 98
Scenario planning, 22
Seiko Watch Company, 68
Service differentiation, 141–2
Service industry attributes, 140
Service industry economies, 139
Service marketing, 139–149
Smith A. E. Ltd, 113–6
Societal marketing, 2
Sociodemographics, 14
Straight line projection, 93
Strategic blindness, 154
Subjective prediction forecast, 93
Suppliers, 20–1
Syndicated research data, 88

Tactical pricing, 80–2
Technological capability, 34–5

Telesales, 101–2
Test market, 55
Time series forecasting, 93
Toshiba, 69
Total quality management, 128–9
Training of marketeers, 161–2
Trustee Savings Bank, 67

UK window frame market, 50–2
Underfunding investments, 103–4
US airline industry, 141–2

Vauxhall cars, 72
Visualization, 62
Vlasic Pickle, 68

Walls Viennetta launch, 73
Warfare management, 65
Wood Care Ltd, 109–113
Working capital, 30
Working in teams, 62–3

Xerox Corporation, 56